Awakening Experience

"Awakening Experience" is a powerful, creative, story about a young woman's struggle with mental illness, her physical journey to gain control over her mind, body and soul. Based from the author's true experiences, dreams and imagination. Full of drama, humor and suspense, designed to entertain you, by Marian Dorsey Copyrights © 1994 and © 1999 by Marian Dorsey All Rights Reserved. Awakening Experience album https://youtu.be/apmPAk-lwWk 1st published Copyrights © 7/5/2011 © 7/24/2020 by Marian Dorsey, Album produced by Adam Ray All Rights Reserved.
"We created my poem Savage Instincts from the Bible. Chapter 4 of Song of Solomon verse 11, Your lips hold the sweet taste of milk and honey". Savage Instincts Lyrics and Music Copyrights ℗ © 2013 by Marian Dorsey featuring Michael J. Williams. Producer Adam Ray and Record by Benj Heard. All Rights Reserved. No parts of this book or recordings may be reproduced, without written notarized permission from the author.
mariandorsey3@aol.com Subject: Requesting Author Permission

Tablet of Content

Awakening Experience……………………….. 2-121

Poems……………………………………………..121-137

Awakening Experience

I can remember when I was about 3 years old. My family lived in a small white house. 2 bedroom and one bathroom in Jackson, Florida. We were surrounded by sweet grass, blackberries, and raspberries. And we had a very old water pump in our front yard. Our pets were several stray dogs, roosters, and chickens. We called the chickens' babies "bitties".

In the beginning of the year when I turned 4, my parents brought a goat we called him Billie. We gave him just about everything to eat so he would be fat, so we could eat him for Christmas. Next to us was a bakery, which all the children in our neighborhood loved to crawl into their dumpster on a regular basis, to eat some of their day-old pastries, cookies and cakes. When we were done eating, we would crawl out with icing all over us.

My name is Marian. I'm the second child in my family. My father James was a cook, in the Army stationed in South Korea. My mother Margaret was a hairdresser. She took good care of Malissa, me and Marbella. Marbella was the baby, always in mama's lap. One day we were all outside in the yard, mama said "come here Marian and see your little sister." My mother knew I never wanted to pay attention to Marbella. She watched how I kept avoiding her. So I walked over to my mother as she sat under a huge pecan tree and looked at Marbella wrapped in a pink blanket. She was so beautiful. I drew my right hand back and slapped her in the face with all my might. I felt jealousy for the first time and I guess that was my first sign of mental illness, a genealogy issue. My mom held Marbella in her left arm while she gave me the spanking of my life with her right hand.

Then a skinny green snake swung from the pecan tree, it caused her to grab my right hand, as she yelled out Malissa! Who had been playing with her wagon in the front yard? We felt our mother's fear, so naturally we were afraid of snakes too. We all ran into the house.

My mother didn't like staying at home waiting for my father. We didn't see him on a regular basis. Sometimes not even for 6 months, we really didn't know when he was coming home, from the Army. So we left the house my father was buying for us. Our mother took us to Brooklyn, New York, to live with her mother. We called Grandma and her family. My two sisters and I had no choice so we soon adjusted well.

My mother loved living in the big city of Brooklyn, New York, where she was raised. My father was so hurt and broken-hearted, he stopped paying on our home. He was in a really bad accident in one of the Army jeeps in South Korea. He suffered from a head concussion and severe depression. And after 6 years in the Army he was given an honorable discharge for medical reasons.

My mother started dating and enjoying the party life with her friends. Leaving us at home with her friends, the neighborhood teenage babysitters or our teenage cousins. Years later we discovered we were abused. Soon my mother became pregnant with my brother Jimmy and a year later my sister Marilyn. Both my parents kept in touch. My father loved our mother so much they both agreed all her children while they were legally married were to be given his last name at birth. They had plans to get back together and be a family, when she discovered she was pregnant again.

So on a Monday night in mid-August 1958, she talked about having an abortion to her girlfriends, who she felt safe with. They team up that night, instead of seeking professional help, pulling out parts of her intestines with an instrument made from a coat hanger. Leaving her baby boy fetus inside of her womb. I know my mother felt a great amount of pain. I can still hear her crying, and screaming and hitting her hand on her bedroom wall, where she suffered for a few days after her friends performed an illegal abortion that cost her, her life.

On Thursday night when my Grandma came home, she discovered her in a drawn up position, in her bed, still crying, and hemorrhaging real bad. Grandma immediately called 911. The paramedics came and took my mother to the hospital. But they arrived too late. My mother died at the age of 26, in the hallway of the hospital. Leaving behind 5 children, my Grandma, my father, and my cousins, who loved her dearly. Her friends who participated, all of them felt sorry and full of regrets, were arrested and jailed.

It was very hard for my grandmother to tell my father. He immediately moved to Brooklyn, New York, to attend her funeral and help my Grandma with raising us. After her funeral he got a job. He did not believe in handouts, he didn't want any help raising us, nor did he want us adopted or separated. His plan was to work until he saved enough money, to move and live with his mother and his family in Los Angeles, California.

When my father was home he taught us how to love one another. He'd say "that's your sister and that's your brother, kiss her, kiss him, hug and hold each other, talk and play games with one another." The most valuable thing of all my father taught us how to pray together, and always tell one another the truth. Through my father we found out Grandma was actually my Biological Maternal aunt, my grandmother's sister. My real grandmother died of pneumonia when my mother was 3 days old, my father said.

We loved Grandma. She worked as a live-in maid for the Bradlaws family in Long Island, New York. She came home every Thursday night, for the weekend. And she would leave on Sunday night. The Bradlaws owned the biggest deli and fish market in

Long Island, New York. She brought home lots of cooked and ready to eat foods: crabs, clams chowder, lobsters, octopus, scallops, shrimps, potatoes salads, macaroni salads, chopped chicken liver, all kinds of bread and pastries we loved to eat. That would last us throughout the week. She worked hard grooming us, braiding, wrapping or curling our hair and taking Jimmy to get his haircut. Then training us how to bathe and prepare our clothes in order for us to look nice in school throughout the week.

    Every Sunday Grandmama took us to church. She was the church treasurer. Me and my siblings sang in the children's choir called the Sunshine Band, at New Jerusalem Baptist Church. Grandma loved fixing up the church. She brought them their first brand new piano with money she had saved from working as a housekeeper. The Pastor was Reverend Thomas Roberts. His wife Mrs. Cindy Roberts was our Sunday School Teacher. They had 5 children, four boys and one girl. I looked forward to going to church. After church, we ate dinner at the Roberts house. Mrs. Roberts and Grandma would let us girls help out, by teaching us how to set the dinner table. Reverend Roberts would tell us bible stories, lead us in prayer and watch us children, as we played games. He was the first pastor to baptize me and my siblings. I can still close my eyes and see Mrs. Roberts playing the piano, her children and the choir singing at my mother's funeral. The Roberts family will always be extra special to me.

Growing up and establishing my identity was hard for me. I've always wanted to be and look different. I tried doing things to hide my pain about losing my mother and being raised in a poor and broken home. I really felt ashamed, cursed and I hated myself deep inside. I wanted it all to go away.

One day my father told us he and his mother had finally saved enough money for our tickets. Which they had already purchased for us to move to Los Angeles, California. We were set to leave on October

31,1963, Halloween night at 11 p.m. on the Greyhound bus. That would be the last night we could go trick or treating with our friends and say goodbye to Grandmama. I was sadder than ever, with thoughts of moving so far from Brooklyn. I didn't want to leave my Grandma, my cousins and friends. But I soon realized that as we grow older, we have to move on with our lives. No one stays the same. There's one thing for sure, we are all going to die, we just don't know when and we don't know how. Life has its own way of ending.

    We left Brooklyn, New York, at the end of my fifth grade semester. I was eleven years old when we arrived in Los Angeles, California. My favorite relatives were my father's mother we called Grandma Bell, her sister Aunt Coulda and her husband Big Daddy. Aunt Coulda and Big Daddy took me into their home for a while. She had a lot of rules: no smoking, no drinking alcoholic beverages, no dancing, no profanity, no! tight clothing, no rhythm & blues, just gospel music and if you were a girl no pants, girl dresses only. Because they live the holy life. But every day they watched General Hospital, Days of Our Lives and One Life to Live. Aunt Coulda would make their doctors' appointments so they would not miss the soap operas. She dipped Bitter Garrett snuff, and chewed tobacco since the age of 10.

    Aunt Coulda made her own cough medicine, to give you for a cold or the flu. Homemade hot tardy! She'd mixed it in a medium pot; 8 ounces of Rum, 4 ounces lemon juice, a half stick of butter and 4 ounces of honey. After it simmered for about 5 minutes and cooled down, she would give you a tablespoon every 4 hours. Until you were healed. They were also the #1 Foster Parent in South Central Los Angeles. And a pair of the world's best cooks.

    On Saturday night Aunt Coulda washed and hard pressed my hair. Oh! How nice I would look after she got me ready for church. While pressing my hair, she talked about her younger days. How she loves to drink, dance and fight. She said somebody had to be talking about you, to know you were talking about them. So bring it on, because she never backs down from a fight. I loved her dearly. Some weeknights, Big Daddy would take me to work with him to the restaurant where he was the janitor. I would wipe the tables and counters. For my lunch he allowed me to make a root beer float with one scoop of ice cream and a cherry on top. And when I finished helping him wipe the tables and counters, he would pay me with some of the extra-large day old cookies and pastries the owner would leave out for him to take home.

    Big Daddy was a hardworking man and very nice to me. I looked at him as if he was one of my grandfathers, instead of an uncle. Because I never met my grandfathers. I only heard stories about them. My father's father was an Indian, who made hair grease out of earthworms. He had to leave Florida running because he killed a white man, for beating him with a whip. No one knows where he ran to or whether he got caught and killed.

My mother's father was an upper class married man. Who didn't want to own her, nor did he want his family to know he cheated on his wife and a child was conceived.

I loved living in Aunt Coulda and Big Daddy house. But most of all I loved to listen to all kinds of music. I believe it's a gift from the good spirits. And I loved to dance too. I couldn't do the tobacco and snuff. I tried, but it was awful to me. And I love tight clothing. These things I loved most were against Aunt Coulda's rules. So I had to move on.

I went to live with Grandma Bell. I loved her too, but things didn't work out well there either. We went to church but it wasn't like New Jerusalem Baptist Church and after going to dinner at the Roberts house. So I didn't like going. Grandma Bell didn't understand my fast nature. All I cared about was, I loved wearing short dresses that would allow my ruffled lace petti pants to show. I loved running after boys. And I loved to chew and pop my bubble gum out loud.

Grandma Bell would complain by saying when I was young, whores dressed like you like to dress and chewed their gum loudly to attract men customers. So don't do that in my house or around me, Marian! She yelled. We had a lot of misunderstandings. She would starch my dresses and put them in the refrigerator until they were damp and cold. Then she'd take them out and iron them.

One day I decided to let my lace petti pants hang from under my dress. It looked pretty to me. But my grandmother didn't like it. So she warned me to pull them up several times before leaving the house. I pulled them up and as soon as I walked out of the house and thought she wasn't looking. I pulled them back down so they can show outside below my dress. Grandma Bell came running out of the house so fast and pulled my dress up and ripped off my lace petti pants. Before the other children that were playing outside. I was so embarrassed. Grandma Bell didn't look at the style on me as being fashionable or pretty. She just thought whores, women of the streets, back in her days liked that type of style for attention to attack men customers. And she wasn't going to have me dressing like them.

A few months passed and I was living in my father's house. My father worked all the time and when he was off, he was an alcoholic. He said he drank to relieve the pain, about the love he had for my mother. He couldn't forget it. And the sadness of not being able to find another mother for us. He was lonely too. It took years for my father to recover from grieving and drinking. We felt his love, but we needed more of him to be a better father to us.

So after school I started having boys in our house and out of our house before my father came home from work. My sisters and brother didn't like it. But they had friends coming in and out too. One thing led to another and I found myself sexually active at 13. Pregnant at 14, a baby at 15 and married at 16. Both of us were still trying to finish school. He was attending in the daytime and I was attending at night. Because we could not afford a babysitter.

When I was 18, he was 19 we had 2 children we discovered were very unhappy. So we filed for a divorce. I was very young and I needed a fresh start. So it was easy for me to move on with my life. I believe you should get to know what a person is really about. Before criticizing them for what they do, I'm not perfect. But I felt I was being judged and criticized, for starting out so young.

As I grew into womanhood rapidly, I only entered into more hardship. Only a few months after being single, I found myself in a very abusive relationship. We fought just about every week and I was pregnant again. I realized I could not re-raise a full grown man, nor could I make him love me. So I decided to secretly disappear with my children and move to Oakland,

California without telling the man I was in a relationship with.

Finding a house in Oakland and applying for public assistance was easy for me. But I still wasn't happy with moving there. I'd also started smoking different street Marijuana's and taking Acid tablets better known as hallucinatory drugs like; Orange Sunshine; Window Pane and Cartoon Acid. And I was pregnant again. Those nine months went by very fast.

All I could think about was I wanted to be loved and happy. As soon as my 4th child was born. Someone gave me some drugs that were laced. I started hearing voices, telling me, "I'm going to wash you and make you clean." I was washing myself 3 to 4 times a day. I was washing everything in my house 3 to 4 times a day and I was washing my children 3 to 4 times a day.

During that time a lady, who was a Jehovah Witness, came to my house and started bible study, 2 times a week. I was mentally unbalanced. I would tear out bible pages, then twist them and tie them around my hair that had Dread locked. And I would put pieces of bible pages in my ears to calm down the voices inside my head. The only way I could sleep was to put my bible in my bed and lay my head in the middle of it. I lived in Oakland, less than 2 years. Because I didn't trust anyone.

      On the last Saturday in July of 1976, I remember cleaning and locking up my house I rented. Taking all my money out of the bank. Then me and my 4 children got on a Greyhound bus back to Los Angeles, California. While riding on the bus I started hearing voices I'd never heard before, telling me I was going to be killed. Get off Now! I had no idea why the voices were telling me that. I just kept praying so loud the bus driver said I was disturbing everyone on the bus. Maybe I needed to get off the bus and get some rest. He said my next stop will be Bakersfield, California. Before I got off the bus, the bus driver tore off a portion of our tickets. So I could get back on another

Greyhound bus, after I get some rest. I didn't know anyone in Bakersfield. So me and my children just started walking around. Then we finally stopped at a grocery store, to get something to eat. After that we walked to a park and stopped for a while. We ate and I let them play for a while.

As the evening approached we started walking again, into the night. Until I heard a voice say stop here!, you can sleep now. We were tired and we'd walked over 30 blocks away from the Greyhound station. To a motel that had a big star in the front of it. We walked inside and there stood a lady from India. She said you need a room for yourself and your children. I said yes! She charged me $36.00 for the night. And lead me into a room with 2 beds and a bathroom. I locked us in and we went to bed. But before the night was up those voices had me washing myself and my children all over again. Several hours passed then finally I was able to get some sleep.

In the morning while checking out I asked the lady from India to call my Aunt Coulda. Aunt Coulda was also a Missionary. She had powerful prayer partners. I spoke to her and asked her to pray for me, so that me and my 4 children could safely return to my father's house. She said yes! Then me and my children walked to a restaurant for breakfast. After breakfast we walked back to the Greyhound bus station. We were able to get back on the Greyhound bus with the rest of our tickets.

I arrived at the Los Angeles Greyhound station wet. Soaking wet from washing myself on the bus. And I had Bible pages all over me. Aunt Coulda, 5 missionaries, my father, my cousin Gloria, met me at the bus terminal. And took me straight to Martin Luther Psychiatric Hospital, for an evaluation. I was there overnight. I asked the doctor please! Don't tell my father I had drugs in my system. I didn't want my father to become an alcoholic again worrying about me. So the doctor said he told my father I had overworked myself and I was suffering from Schizophrenia. I was released and prescribed some Valiums, and sleeping pills.

My father had me and my children living at his house for two months. I didn't have a job or any kind of public assistance. So I pawned my necklaces, earrings and wedding ring set. When my money was spent I went and applied for public assistance. I gave them copies of my medical records from the hospital. And I told them everything I had been through. I have 4 children. I was divorced. I did not want to smoke any more street Marijuana or take any hallucinated drugs. I did not want to hear any more voices and I suffer from schizophrenia. Fortunately I had a Social Worker that listened. And I knew I wasn't ready to go to work.

So my Social Worker asked me if I want to continue living with my father. I said yes! She issued me an emergency check to help me and some food stamps. And told me they would be coming on a monthly basis, until I get a job. I told her, I'd pay them back, someday. She laughed and said, Okay! Public Assistance is here to help people who need it.

    I always paid my bills on time. But my life was just turning into a nightmare. It seemed like everything that I liked to do the most, the voices I heard were taking me away. And I knew I needed help. My children kept me strong. I did not want to ever leave them. Because I didn't want them to have a childhood like mine. I wanted to become a better mother. At my father's house, he did most of the cooking. It wasn't long before I started eating a lot of healthy foods: fresh fruits, vegetables, chicken, turkey, veal, fish, beef, rice and noodles. I tried not to eat pork, nothing but bacon. I also drank a lot of fruit juices, plenty of water and I started taking good multiple vitamins.

    Then I started going to a group mental therapy class, 2 times a week. While my children were in school. And the best thing that could have happened to me, was I met a lady who was a guest speaker Mrs. Dora Smith. She talked about God to my class. Then she invited me and my children to her church. I learned to understand the voices that I was hearing. The evil voices and which were the good voices. That led me away from becoming a drug addict. My whole life changed. I even finished high school. I got a job as a telephone operator and I started Freelance writing in my spare time. My first book was a scripted play. I started feeling good about myself. I wanted the world to know I exist.

"Deposition of an Awakening Experience"

Marian: It's Tuesday, 7 July, 1992 10:00 a.m. Mr. Biloba was my attorney. Mr. De Aloes was the attorney for the defendant, Eden, a company I'd previously worked for. I was called as witness on behalf of the defendant, having been first duly sworn, was examined and testified as follows:

Mr. De Aloes: May I have your full name for the record, please?

Marian Dorsey!

Mr. De Aloes: Do you have a middle name?

Marian: No!

Mr. De Aloes: And is Dorsey a married name or maiden name?

Marian: Maiden name

Mr. De Aloes: Have you ever gone by any other name?

Marian: Yes! I've been married twice. One dissolution and one annulment. So they didn't stick.

Mr. De Aloes: And what were your two prior married names?

Marian: The dissolution was first, when I was eighteen I was Hayes, H-a-y-e-s. The annulment was from Burns, B-u-r-n-s. I was twenty-four.

Mr. De Aloes: Have you ever had your deposition taken before?

Marian: No! I've never had a deposition before.

Mr. De Aloes: Did you spend some time with your attorney discussing the deposition process?

Marian: Yes!

Mr. De Aloes: How much time did you spend with your attorney?

Marian: I believe it was over an hour.

Mr. De Aloes Talking solely about what happens in a deposition?

Marian: Yes! And how I felt

Mr. Biloba: Counsel for the record, applicants counsel will stipulate to exactly thirty minutes in preparation time as being reasonable.

Mr. De Aloes: Okay! I'm sure your attorney explained all the do's and don'ts about a deposition and the rules. I'm going to make sure that you understand some of the more basic things. The person seated to my left is a certified shorthand reporter. Everything you say here today she will record and later on transcribe into a booklet. That booklet will be sent to your attorney's office, who will then have the responsibility of contacting you so you will have an opportunity to make any changes or corrections to your testimony that you deem are necessary. If you make any changes to your story, as opposed to spelling or grammatical changes it may affect your credibility and the judge may not believe you; and so for that reason, I ask that you think about the questions that I pose and think about your answers before giving me the answer. If you have any questions about your answers· or questions about the questions that I pose, then let me know so that those can be restated. Okay?

Marian: Uh Huh!

Mr. De Aloes: The court reporter also issued you an oath. That means you're testifying under penalty of perjury and that requires you to testify truthfully. Do you understand that?

Marian: Yes!

Mr. De Aloes: Are you on any drugs or medication at this time?

Marian: No!

Mr. De Aloes: Is there any reason why you would not be able to testify competently?

Marian: No! I have nothing to hide. I will answer as it comes to my mind. (*I sat calmly as this strange feeling overtook me.*)

Mr. De Aloes: What is your date of birth?

Marian: Ten, ten, fifty-two

Mr. De Aloes: And where were you born?

Marian: Florida

Mr. De Aloes: When did you move to California?

Marian: I first moved to California in November of 1963.

Mr. De Aloes: Have you lived in California ever since then?

Marian: Yes! I have left several times and went to New York and back to California.

Mr. De Aloes: When was the last time that you came back to California from New York?

Marian: Oh! Well, I have also been to Washington.

Mr. De Aloes: When is the last time that you left?

Marian: I left and came back in 1987. I went to Washington, No! I'm sorry! Take that back. Not 1987, but 1988.

Mr. De Aloes: (*lifting his eyebrows upon his forehead saying in a heavy curious voice*) And you went to Washington?

Marian: Yes! I went to Washington, then Lynwood.

Mr. De Aloes: Then when did you return to California?

Marian: I stayed there for six weeks, so it was still in 1988.

Mr. De Aloes: Your counsel has presented me with a photocopy of your driver's license. Let me show that to you.

Marian: Yes!

Mr. De Aloes: That's correct! Is that photocopy a correct reproduction of yours?

Marian: Yes!

Mr. De Aloes: Driver's license?

Marian: Yes!

Mr. De Aloes: Does anybody live with you at your current address?

Marian: Yes! My daughter Mynisha Lawrence.

Mr. De Aloes: How do you spell that?

Marian: L-a-w-r-e-n-c-e

Mr. De Aloes: L-a-w-r-e-n-c-e?

Marian: Yes! Lawrence

Mr. De Aloes: Okay!

Marian: *(I felt he didn't trust me as I stated her first name)* Mynisha, M-y-n-i-s-h-a.

Mr. De Aloes: Okay!

Marian: And she is sixteen and my son.

Mr. De Aloes: Uh Huh!

Marian: He lives with me in and out. His name is Nathaniel Gaverett, G-a-v-e-r-e-t-t.

Mr. De Aloes: And how old is he?

Marian: He is nineteen.

Mr. De Aloes: Anybody else live with you?

Marian: I wouldn't call it living with me, he comes and goes spending some time at his grandmother's house.

Mr. De Aloes: Do you have others who?

Marian: Yes! I have others who visit and spend the night. But nobody that calls the place home so to speak? Yes! My apartment is a cooling place for some kids. They come over for a week or 2 and stay until their parents and the child come to an agreement.

Mr. De Aloes: Do you have an automobile?

Marian: Yes!

Mr. De Aloes: How many?

Marian: One!

Mr. De Aloes: And what kind is it?

Marian: 1980 Toyota Tercel, five speed.

Mr. De Aloes: What color is it?

Marian: Rusty Red.

Mr. De Aloes: Do you know the license plate number?

Marian: I have to look for it. Wait a minute. I don't have the license plate number with me.

Mr. De Aloes: Did you drive here today?

Marian: No!

Mr. De Aloes: How did you get here today?

Marian: My attorney Mr. Biloba drove me here with him this morning.

Mr. De Aloes: What's the highest grade of education you've achieved?

Marian: Well I went to twelfth grade, but I took my G.E.D. test. I've also spent a year and a half in college.

Mr. De Aloes: Where did you attend college?

Marian: Daniel Freeman College, San Pablo, California. And I also took a class at the university extension.

Mr. De Aloes: When did you attend college,

Marian: Daniel Freeman College? I think it was in 1987.

Mr. De Aloes: And then you took?

Marian: I also attended another college too.

Mr. De Aloes: Do you recall where? Las Cascara College Where is that located?

Marian: Pittsburg, California

Mr. De Aloes: And when did you go there?

Marian: I believe it was '84.

Mr. De Aloes: Did you obtain any degrees or certificates of completion from these colleges?

Marian: No! No! Why are we going around in circles again?

Mr. De Aloes: Okay! I'm just trying to get clear statements from you, Marian!

Marian: Well I have grades, not a degree yet.

Mr. De Aloes: Then when did you take the university extension courses?

Marian: Last semester I took one course.

Mr. De Aloes: What course was that?

Marian: Becoming a recording artist. Music was my major.

Mr. De Aloes: And what university did you take that extension course from?

Marian: The last class at the university extension? I found my license plate.

Mr. De Aloes: Okay. What's your license plate number?

Marian: 2BKS845.

Mr. De Aloes: Thank you!

Marian: You're welcome!

Mr. De Aloes: Have you ever served in the military?

Marian: No!

Mr. De Aloes: Have you ever been convicted of a felony?

Marian: No! I've never been arrested.

Mr. De Aloes: Have you ever filed a workers compensation claim in the past?

Marian: No! Never

Mr. De Aloes: Have you ever filed for state disability in the past?

Marian: ummm Not in the past, Just recently.

Mr. De Aloes: Just in connection with this case?

Marian: Yes!

Mr. De Aloes: Who certified you for disability with regards to this case?

Marian: When you say "who certified me," what are you-talking about? What do you mean?

Mr. De Aloes: Did a doctor say that you were disabled?

Marian: Yes!

Mr. De Aloes: What doctor?

Marian: I first went to Stress Care. I don't have the doctor's name. Then I went to Sheffield Medical Center. Dr. Stewart, that's the one I saw the most. At Stress Care I went through psychotherapy with Joanna. I don't know her last name. And at Sheffield Medical with Dr. Stewart was for.... physical therapy.

Mr. De Aloes: Do you know when your disability began? In other words, when did you start receiving disability payments?

Marian: Now wait a minute, I have not received a disability payment yet, from Eden!

Mr. De Aloes: So then, they just recently certified you for state disability, Right?

Marian: No! I have not received state disability. I have the last letter from Goldenseal Insurance I bought that with me stating why they did not send my disability.

Mr. Biloba: Counsel for the record, Ms. Dorsey is unable to get state disability because of the private program I believe that Eden has for disability with Goldenseal Insurance.

Mr. De Aloes: Okay! The witness has generated a letter dated May 21,1992 from the Goldenseal Insurance Company signed by Deborah Jeremiah, J-e-r-e-m-i-a-h.

Counsel, do you have any objection to attaching that as an exhibit to the deposition transcript?

Mr. Biloba: None whatsoever. So stipulated.

Marian: Here is another one.

Mr. De Aloes: The important part in the letter basically states that disability provided through The Goldenseal would not be commenced because-or it says, quote, No coverage is supplied while you are on leave without pay, end quote. Have the court reporter make a copy of that.

Marian: And here is another one. I called state disability on this one and this is what they mailed me.

Mr. De Aloes: That's fine,

Marian: Thank you!. She wrote another one on June the fifth.

Mr. De Aloes: So you made an application for disability through Eden. Correct?

Marian: Yes!

Mr. De Aloes: Now do you understand the difference between disability through Eden, and what I mean when we say state disability?

Marian: Well, the state wrote me back and said that they could not help me because Eden was privately owned. The letter stated that they don't take out state disability. They have their own disability.

Mr. De Aloes: So you received a letter from the Disability office? Employment- from the EDD office?

Marian: Yes!

Mr. Biloba: I believe Eden's, in her paychecks, withholds nothing for SDI, so I believe it's inapplicable.

Mr. De Aloes: Oh! Okay, that's fine. Have you ever been involved in any motor vehicle accidents?

Marian: Yes!

Mr. De Aloes: How many?

Marian: Well, I was involved in a motorcycle accident. I believe it was....I was involved in two.

Mr. De Aloes: When was the most recent one?

Marian: 1976!

Mr. De Aloes: And when was the...one before the last one?

Marian: No! There was one before that. It was in '73 and that's the only two, 1976 and 1973.

Mr. De Aloes: Did you receive any injuries as a result of this motor vehicle accident?

Marian: Yes! In 1973.

Mr. De Aloes: What kind of injuries did you sustain?

Marian: Neck and back injuries.

Mr. De Aloes: Did you receive medical treatment for those injuries?

Marian: Yes! I was in the hospital for about a week.

Mr. De Aloes: What hospital?

Marian: I don't remember the name of the hospital.

Mr. De Aloes: Do you recall where it was located?

Marian: No!

Mr. De Aloes: What kind of treatment did you get in 1973 for your neck injuries?

Marian: They put a neck brace on Uhum! And I believe it was heat medication and they also gave me massages for my neck and back.

Mr. De Aloes: Anything else? Any other treatment?

Marian: No! I can't remember anything else.

Mr. De Aloes: Did you get any… or ..did you sustain any injuries as a result of your 1976 automobile accident?

Marian: No! *(Mr. De Aloes is getting on my nerves)*

Mr. De Aloes: Have you ever been involved in a lawsuit in the past?

Marian: No!

Mr. De Aloes: Have you ever made a claim against anybody or any entity for personal injuries in the past?

Marian: No!

Mr. De Aloes: You're not currently married Correct?

Marian: Correct! I'm not currently married.

Mr. De Aloes: You have been married twice before. Correct?

Marian: Yes! When I turned fifteen and again when I turned twenty-four.

Mr. De Aloes: When did the last marriage end?

Marian: You want the date of the final? The nullity date when I filed it or the date when it ended? Like when we said, "I do," and then it ended in nullity?

Mr. De Aloes: Let's have an approximate date of whenever the final decree was entered by the court?

Marian: Okay! I believe it was, I don't have the papers with me.

Mr. De Aloes: Give me an approximate date.

Marian: 76. '76 or '77 it was final, but I do believe it was '76. Wait a minute; let me think, July 12, 1976.

Mr. De Aloes: And which marriage was that, the divorce or the annulment?

Marian: 1976 was an annulment

Mr. De Aloes: What were the grounds for annulment?

Marian: I don't know what the grounds were ahuh! irreconcilable differences.

Mr. De Aloes: Irreconcilable differences?

Marian: Yes! That's the word.

Mr. De Aloes: And then you were married before then, also?

Marian: Yes!

Mr. De Aloes: When did that first marriage end?

Marian: Well! That was from the ninth grade to the twelfth grade. After the twelfth grade it ended. It lasted three years and on August 14,1975 the divorce was final.

Mr. De Aloes: Did these marriages produce any children?

Marian: Yes! The first marriage did. The second one, I was already pregnant. My first child was born before my first marriage.

Mr. De Aloes: Who was the child by the first marriage?

Marian: Flawn'Telle Hayes. I was pregnant with her when I was fourteen.

Mr. De Aloes: How do you spell Flawn'Telle?

Marian: Flawn'Telle, F -l-a-w-n apostrophe, capital T-e-l-l-e. And Lishelle, L-i-s-h-e-l-l- e, Hayes. I was seventeen when she was born.

Mr. De Aloes: How old is Flawn'Telle?

Marian: She is twenty-five and Lishelle is twenty-three.

Mr. De Aloes: Where do they currently reside?

Marian: Flawn'Telle lives in Long Island, Queens, New York. Lishelle lives in Wilmington, Delaware.

Mr. De Aloes: And you indicated that you were already pregnant for the second marriage, is that correct?

Marian: Yes! I was already pregnant when I got married, about six months.

Mr. De Aloes: Who was the child of that marriage?

Marian: My marriage with David Burns

Mr. De Aloes: Yes! Is Mynisha also part of that marriage?

Marian: No! David Burns was not her father. Mynisha is Jeff Lawrence's child.

Mr. De Aloes: Wait a second. I think I'm a little confused here. Jeff is Mynisha's father. and Mynisha is sixteen.

Marian: No! She will be seventeen in December.

Mr. De Aloes: So who was the child that you were pregnant with at the time of your second marriage?

Marian: Mynisha! Jeff Lawrence was the father of my child.

Mr. De Aloes: Of Mynisha?

Marian: Yes! Okay, I said it that's right.this time

Mr. De Aloes: So Jeff was the husband?

Marian: He wasn't the husband.

Mr. De Aloes: Well! The- The lover, the first father?

Marian: Oh No! He was the third father, because Nathaniel Gaverett Senior is my son's father.

Mr. De Aloes: So there are three different fathers Morris Haynes, Nathaniel Gaverett Senior, Jeff Lawrence

Marian: I've known Morris Haynes since we were in elementary school.

Mr. De Aloes: Wait a second. What I want to do here is to get all this straight, because you know more about this than I do. Okay! And it will be confusing if you try to explain it to me all at once. You have three men that have fathered your 4 children, Right?

Marian: Yes!

Mr. De Aloes: Who is the first father?

Marian: Morris Hayes! He produced Flawn'Telle and Lishelle Okay! The second father is? Nathaniel Gaverett Senior, he used to be our paperboy. I would smooch him. You know kiss, grind and have sex with him to keep the money my father would give me to pay for our monthly newspapers. I was thirteen. Luckily I didn't get pregnant then.

Mr. De Aloes: Oh! And he produced?

Marian: Nathaniel Gaverett Jr., which is my third child. He was born when I was twenty. Okay! And then the third father is Jeff Lawrence. And that's Mynisha's father

Mr. De Aloes: Okay, do I have all of your kids now?

Marian: Yes! Mynisha, Nathaniel? Are still in the home.

Mr. De Aloes: I'm sorry

Marian: For what? Mynisha and Nathaniel are still in the home. Flawn'Telle and Lishelle live back East, I don't why you're sorry.

Mr. De Aloes: Okay! Are you currently cohabiting with anybody at this time?

Marian: No. I've been single since September. The first week of September. Of 91?

Mr. De Aloes: Was somebody living with you?

Marian: *(I was thinking to myself you are so dumb! As I inhaled a deep breath)* Jeff Lawrence! Jeff was living with me!

Mr. De Aloes: Where does he live now?

Marian: I don't have the slightest idea.

Mr. De Aloes: Are you currently employed?

Marian: Yes! With Eden telecommunications.

Mr. De Aloes: Are you currently working there?

Marian: No! My last day of work was on April the ninth. April tenth I filed for job stress.

Mr. De Aloes: Four, nine, ninety-two was the last day that you worked?

Marian: Yes!

Mr. De Aloes: What did you do in telecommunications; what was your job?

Marian: I answered the S L I00. It's a computerized Centrex phone system. And in rotation, I worked the front desk. I also delivered the mail, in rotation. And I worked special assignments, on the... on the telephone what was it called? Oh, I can't think.. TSR's!

Mr. De Aloes: What is a TSR?

Marian: That's when you make corrections, you make sure that the disconnected numbers are disconnected and find out what is the new number, or where to transfer the calls to.

Mr. De Aloes: So basically it manages the computerized phone system?

Marian: Yes! You call other departments clarifying the new number or where to transfer
the calls to.

Mr. De Aloes: When did you start working for Eden? October the twenty-second, 1990.

Marian: And what was your, what's your pay? $1,917 a month. That's my pay now.

Mr. De Aloes: So you're a salaried employee, then?

Marian: Yes!

Mr. De Aloes: Did you get paid for overtime?

Marian: Yes!

Mr. De Aloes: What do you get paid for overtime?

Marian: I don't know about the overtime. I only worked overtime once, and that was on a Saturday with the resident halls. Enrolling in the new telephone numbers for the new students.

Mr. De Aloes: Would you describe your job at Eden as basically a desk job?

Marian: Yes! It's basically a desk job.

Mr. De Aloes: Who is your supervisor there?

Marian: Well, they had Kathy as my acting supervisor. And the manager is Agnes Bilberry, I think that's it.

Mr. De Aloes: How did you describe him, again? What was his-?

Marian: It's a she, Agnes? Agnes, yes! B-i-l-b-e-r-r-y, I believe it's spelled.

Mr. De Aloes: What was her capacity? And who did you report to?

Marian: Kathy!

Mr. De Aloes: Do you know her last name?

Marian: Yes! I've got it down here. Uhumm What's her name? Here it is. The acting supervisor is Kathy. Kathy Papayas, P-a-p-a-y-a-s. She is the acting supervisor. Okay!

Mr. De Aloes: So you answered the phones on the Centrex system full-time. Correct? In other words, that was basically your job?

S L l00 Telephone operator, job title principal clerk. Right! Then along with other employees you alternated with regards to working the front desk and delivering mail. Correct?

Marian: Yes! And cleaning up the kitchen.on certain days, certain times of the month, it was our department who cleaned the kitchen.

Mr. De Aloes: How many people did you rotate with, with regards to working the front desk?

Marian: Well, I believe all the operators except the ones that weren't trained.

Mr. De Aloes: Can you take a guess?

Marian: Well, I don't want to guess,

Mr. De Aloes: Okay! How about an educated estimate?

Marian: I believe all of them. I would say eight. Eight of them? Yes! rotated with regards to delivering the mail? And No! I have not seen everyone deliver the mail.

Mr. De Aloes: How many do you think you rotated with for delivering the mail?

Marian: I don't want to tell a lie. I don't know. Less than eight, more than five? Probably about five. Okay! Because some of them would refuse to do it.

Mr. De Aloes: Who refused to do it?

Marian: At first Linda didn't deliver the mail at all, because she said it bothered her back. And neither did oh, what's her name? There's another lady's name that I don't remember. It bothered her back sometimes too. I can't think of her name, but some of the old operators who had back problems, the students would deliver the mail for them or the supervisor would assign someone. Doris was another one, it bothered her back, she wouldn't do it. And sometimes they called me to another department to help out because I was a very good worker. I would go in and help with the process of the phone bills. You know, I've been around ... Rebecka has called me into her office to help, but when it's busy they can't call me. I would feed the computer the new telephone numbers. I also got the phone bills together and sent them out to their departments. And I took the mail over to the mailroom, and sorted the mail.

Mr. De Aloes: Who would ask you to do all of this job?

Marian: Sorting the mail would be a part of the assignment for the front desk. But to work on the telephone projects, with the telephone bill, it would be Rebecka.

Mr. De Aloes: Do you know Rebecca's last name?

Marian: Calvin, C-a-l-v-i-n and sometimes everybody would take a turn and come into the big conference room to separate the bills. Certain times of the semester, when the new students come in, we have a whole lot of bills and payments with different departments. We met in a conference room and everybody would be assigned a box, and that box would have several telephone bills, inventory slips and payment receipts, over 30 pounds. We'd put each person or department telephone bill and inventory slips into envelopes and sealed them. Then put them into another box to be delivered to that department.

Mr. De Aloes: Where did you work before Eden? Did you have a job title?

Marian: Yes! I worked at the Medfly hotline. As an operator with the Medfly project.

Mr. De Aloes: When did you work that job?

Marian: Oh, I have it all in my head. It was an Agriculture Aide 1500 hours project seasonal job. I got hired in '89. I believe it was November until August '90. Then I transferred to another department.

Mr. De Aloes: What department of the government ran the Medfly hotline?

Marian: The Agricultural Department ran the medfly project otherwise known as the Mediterranean fruit fly project. The medfly is a pest that is capable of causing extensive damage to a wide range of fruit crops. In The United States especially California. Well, I have a card here. Let's see. I believe it was The State Agricultural Commissioners, that's where I went. This is where I first went for employment. Okay! Mr. Pearson was the one that hired me, but later on other supervisors took over.

Mr. De Aloes: The witness has produced a business card from the Office of Agricultural Commissioner, Weights and Measures, County of Los Angeles here in California.

Marian: Yes! In EL Monte. California. I was there for about three months. And then we moved over into trailers in EL Monte.

Mr. De Aloes: What did you do for the job, or that project?

Marian: The first four months I answered the medfly hotline, for the television commercial that gave out information on the aerial sprayings. The fly trappings, the results of the spray, any effect on a person, car or home. And the location of the spraying that would be for that night. Then in the last three months, they put me on rotation with two other employees. Releasing medflies, navigating, and driving. And we also filled the trucks with buckets of medflies which we released in assigned locations, in Los Angeles County.

Mr. De Aloes: Why did that employment end?

Marian: It was just seasonal 1500 hours. It was classified as a state emergency.

Mr. De Aloes: Did you ever get injured doing that job?

Marian: No! The buckets of medflies were very very light. The treatment was to release the sterile medflies, so when they mate, they wouldn't reproduce. When we released a bucket of medflies, we wore gargles to protect our eyes. A jumpsuit covered our clothes and we had a mask over our mouth. Otherwise, the flies would go into our nose and everything. The state trucks were kept in excellent condition. But talking on the telephones, answering the public questions took a very long time. I worked a lot of overtime there.. When they sprayed, they didn't spray us. I was never around while they were spraying. And as a matter of fact, when they did spray my area, I left and went over to my sisters house. When they sprayed her area, she would come to my apartment.

Mr. De Aloes: Did you have any employment in between the end of your job at the medfly hotline and the beginning of your job at Eden?

Marian: No! I didn't have any employment between them.

Mr. De Aloes: Did you have any source of income between that period and now?

Marian: Well, I received unemployment and AFDC supplements.

Mr. De Aloes: Did you have a job prior to working for the medfly hotline?

Marian: Yes! Shemeric Answering Service.

Mr. De Aloes: How do you spell that?

Marian: S-h-e-m-e-r-i-c, Shemeric. Which was run by Mariah Garcia, but it's now out of business. She went out of business because she was losing her eyesight.

Mr. De Aloes: What were your dates of employment at Shemeric Answering Service?

Marian: It was part-time, mostly on the weekends, from four o'clock to twelve o'clock and on call. I also worked upstairs on the seventeenth floor part-time with Mr. Richard Samuel, motorcycle accidents insurance attorney.

Mr. De Aloes: He specialized in motorcycle accidents?

Marian: Yes! And I had one more. I was doing three jobs. The other one was working at Figma, a company that made hard disks. I worked at the front desk.

Mr. De Aloes: You worked these three jobs concurrently. Right?

Marian: Yes!

Mr. De Aloes: What's the address of Mr. Samuel's office?

Marian: Seventeen! hundred.. I don't know. Seventeen something Ventura. It's in Encino on Ventura Blvd. I don't quite remember if it was 1710 something. Shemeric and Mr. Samuel were in the same building. And Figma was about 5 miles away in Reseda on Derby Avenue. Before that I was at The School District, working on call with special children, in northern California. I I lived in Richmond California then.

Mr. De Aloes: When did you work for the schools?

Marian: Well, I worked there as a substitute instructional aide and volunteer and I started there in September 1983.

Mr. De Aloes: When did you last worked there

Marian: June 1987

Mr. De Aloes: And in 1987 you moved back to Southern California?

Marian: Yes!

Mr. De Aloes: Why did you move back to Southern California in 1987?

Marian: Well! After my aunt died.

Mr. De Aloes: I'm sorry?

Marian: After the death of my aunt, who lived in Oakland, I wanted to get closer to my sister. I wanted to make up to her, show her I love her. When she was in the 3rd grade and I was in the 4th grade. I burned her because she started hitting me for taking so long ironing. I had just woken up and I didn't realize I'd retaliated by holding the iron against her breast. My Grandma whipped me so badly about that. I ran out of the house all the way to school in my pajamas to get away from Grandma's hard slaps in my face. And I stayed at school until my father came to pick me up.

When I was 3 years old I even slapped her, because she was always in my mother's arms. I didn't want my sister to think I was possessed by a demon, Uh um maybe I was. But I really wanted her to get to know me. Cause I love my sisters. To this day I regret those things I did to her. I'm hoping and praying one day she'll forgive me.

Mr De Aloes: Your other sisters lived down here?

Marian: Yes! I have one sister and a brother who lives in Los Angeles and my oldest sister lives in San Bernardino. We fought all the time too, just not as severe. Then I have

some cousins that live here also. But I don't know them well. Oh! My youngest sister lives in Brooklyn, New York.

Mr. De Aloes: Did you ever get injured working for... how do you pronounce that answering service, again?

Marian: Shemeric.

Mr. De Aloes: Did you ever get injured working for Richard Samuel?

Marian: No!

Mr. De Aloes: And you never got injured working for Figma?

Marian: No!

Mr. De Aloes: Did you ever get injured working for the school district?

Marian: No!

Mr. De Aloes: Why did your employment at Richard Samuel's office end?

Marian: Well! He had a layoff.

Mr. De Aloes: So you got laid off?

Marian: Yes! And how about Figma? I quit!

Mr. De Aloes: Why did you quit?

Marian: I was taken off the front desk. One of my co-workers started training me how to do the company's inventory on the computers. My supervisor did not give me a seat in the back office. So I was sitting down on the floor working, doing inventory, on the computer without a seat or a desk. I came all the way from North Hollywood on the bus! To the city of Reseda to work at

8 a.m. to sit on the floor and work. Until somebody gets up for a break or leaves for lunch. Then I could sit on their seat at their desk and do my work. After 2 weeks I started thinking real funny thoughts.

Mr. De Aloes: Did you ask them for a seat?

Marian: Yes! I was told they would be getting me one and I waited over two weeks.

Mr. De Aloes: You never got a seat from them?

Marian: No!

Mr. De Aloes: So you quit, then right?

Marian: Yes! They tried calling me back, but I told them, No! I would find something else for $6 an hour.

Mr. De Aloes: Was Figma your last job before you went to work on the med fly hotline?

Marian: No! Shemeric was. You see I was working three jobs and then they started laying off. From 8:00 a.m. to 5:00 p.m. Mondays through Fridays, I was at Figma. 5:00 p.m. to 12:00 a.m. on Mondays through Sundays I was working for Shermic Answering Service. I had another operator sit for one hour for me, until I got there. I would pay her for her time, because I would get there a little late. 9 a.m. Saturday and Sunday mornings I was on the seventeenth floor in the Attorney Richard Samuel stuffing letters into envelopes about motorcycle coverage and laws. I worked very hard.

Mr. De Aloes: How did you get injured at Eden?

Marian: Well, it started as a build-up. On May the 8th I started talking to my co-workers in my department that I saw on a regular basis that I was planning to have breast implants. I wanted them inserted under my chest muscles. Because my self- esteem was very low, about my small flat hanging breast, after having 4 children. I didn't like the look I'd developed. So I prepared myself for the operation. I told my supervisors that I would be out over my sick days. So please deduct it from my vacation time. I didn't want the laughter when I came back into the office, we had over ten people in our office and over twenty employed on the same floor. I always talked to everybody as friendly as I could. I'm going to have breast implants hoping they want to know why I am going to be out. Okay! When I came back to work, knowing everyone knew what had happened, there was very little laughter. That didn't bother me or I didn't notice because of the medications I was taking. My supervisor Agnes Bilberry kept asking me to go deliver the mail, by pushing the mail cart. I would think, why does she want me to walk around in all the offices at a time like this? I didn't want to

be doing that so soon. I was just fine sitting there answering the S L-l00 and now, all of a sudden she wants me to push the cart around in and out of these offices taking the mail. Now she is trying, you know, to make a spectacle out of me and this stuff. I was a small 32A and now I'm a large 36C. My stitches burst twice, because I was moving around so much. I had to have the doctor re-stitch the area.

Mr. De Aloes: I'm sorry?

Marian: The doctor said, Maybe it was due to the lace bra and too much moving. And I told him that I was pushing the mail around. Several other supervisors made statements and comments that it was too much for me. And I also told Agnes that it was too much for me, so they took me off delivering the mail.

Mr. De Aloes: Who did your breast implants? Where did you have surgery?

Marian: The plastic surgeons at Eden's Medical Center 800 Med Plaza.

Mr. De Aloes: Was there a particular doctor in charge of your care?

Marian: Oh! It was performed by medical students and intern doctors.

Mr. De Aloes: How was that surgery paid for?

Marian: I paid cash. It was cosmetic surgery. The insurance I had didn't cover any part of it.

Mr. De Aloes: How much did that cost?

Marian: $3,700.

Mr. De Aloes: Did you have to get hospitalized for that?

Marian: No! It was a one day surgery. I came in at 6 a.m. in the morning. I was out by 4 o'clock.

Mr. De Aloes: Then what's the next thing that happened?

Marian: The next thing that happened was, I explained to my supervisor when I was sick to deduct it out of my vacation time, that I had accumulated since May of the previous year. okay! In the month of October I noticed my check was not right, and I didn't say anything. Then, in November I spoke to Peter, he's another supervisor who works in the payroll department. I asked Peter. I want my sick days deducted from my vacation time. And when I noticed it was taken, I had to ask him again. Peter! Why weren't my sick days deducted from my vacation time? I still have vacation time right. Peter said it's not me, it's Kathy.

I said when she comes in, would you please tell her that I would like to speak with her? I want to make sure she understands what I'm asking for.

Mr. De Aloes: I'm not sure how all this works. You'll have to explain it to me again.

Marian: I wanted the 5 extra sick days I was off for my surgery deducted from my 14 days of vacation time.

Mr. De Aloes: Let's say you didn't ask them to deduct it from your vacation time. What is the normal procedure if you're sick?

Marian: They will deduct it from your regular hours. If you go over one sick day a month. You can accumulate 12 sick days a year. And you can have hours or days you're out sick deducted from your vacation time.

Mr. De Aloes: So twelve sick days per year. Right?

Marian: Yes! and 14 vacation days a year.

Mr. De Aloes: Let's say you're not sick for three months and then you get sick; do you get three days-sick days-pay without having any deduction?

Marian: Yes! That's correct.

Mr. De Aloes: Did you have sick days accrued by the time your surgery occurred?

Marian: Yes! I had 12 sick days and 14 vacation days.

Mr. De Aloes: You asked that the remaining absence, or days that you were absent, be deducted from your vacation time. Correct?

Marian: When I came back to work, I still had five more vacation days left. Because I didn't use up all my vacation days. I thought it was Peter in the payroll department messing up things. Kathy wouldn't do this to me. So I asked Kathy and Kathy said, I hadn't been talking to her. I said, what do you want me to say Kathy?" I don't gossip. Kathy also started passing me news paper and magazine clips of articles she read in the paper on breast implants and cancer. I wanted her to stop doing that, because I didn't want to read about cancer and breast implants. So I believe she was kind of upset about that. So she didn't enforce my request.

Mr. De Aloes: I'm just a little bit confused, but it's getting better. I want to make sure I know how much time you took off for your surgery?

Marian: 21 days, But I'd accumulated 12 sick days and 14 vacation days. When I returned to work I had 5 vacation days left. When I needed days off from work, to visit my doctors, I wanted them deducted from my vacation days.

Mr. De Aloes: Was this all related to the surgery? the times you were taking off?

Marian: Yes! I did it that way, so I would have a complete full month's check. *(My thoughts went Wow! There are a lot of questions. I wonder do Mr. De Aloes has an eye for me, does he notice how beautiful I look or is he looking at my breasts? Why is he so nosey about my personal life? All those questions are not job related. But my attorney Mr. Biloba isn't objecting to any of his questions.)*

Mr. De Aloes: Okay!

Marian: I had ordered some vitamins. To come to the office. And someone put "redeliver" to my home address, on the box of vitamins. I've ordered vitamins before and that didn't happen. But this time my vitamins floated in the mail over eleven days. Because someone scribbled out my work address and wrote my address and home phone number on the box. And I...I kept calling the vitamin place and saying, I ordered some vitamins. What happened to my vitamins? The vitamins company usually has them to Eden the second or third day. No one had said anything to me before. They have clothes, food, and perfume delivered to the office. Flowers, bubble gum, all that. I didn't think my vitamins would have offended anyone. When I called the vitamin company they told me, they said, Marian! We sent your vitamins to you at Eden. It had your Eden's address and telephone number on there. I called UPS and they said we went to Eden and someone at Eden told UPS to redeliver my box to my home address. And no one was there. When they came back up to Eden, they kept on rerouting it to my home. So I started questioning all the operators. I said why would ya'll do me like that? I received everything. When y'all husbands called with flowers, Valentine's Day presents, candy, sandwiches, anything that came in here, I called that person and I respect them. I tell them, you have something at the front desk. Why play games with my vitamins? I needed them. If I took my medicine, I'd be sleepy. That's why I ordered vitamins with just a thirty-day supply of vitamin packs, which you can buy over the counter in a drug store. Everybody said, No! but there was still laughter with certain operators in the office. Laughing about me, how I was reacting to my mail and my breast implants. I loved coming to work in tank tops and cat suits without a bra. We didn't have a dress code. Kathy was my supervisor, she was still laughing too. I told her I'm serious and I believed they were jealous. So after that I questioned everyone. I said well, I'm going to talk to Agnes about it. Agnes told me, Marian, I don't want you to have any vitamins delivered here. I said Why? Agnes I don't have chicken, sandwiches, lunch or flowers. I don't have anything else to come in here. She said Well, you're not supposed to have UPS packages come here. I said all you had to do is call me, and I could come to the front desk and sign for it. There's no one at my apartment to get the package for me. I said I believe

Kathy had my package redelivered and put my home phone number and address on it. This is the reason why because she said I wasn't talking to her as a friend anymore. Agnes started laughing but what was funny? What was funny to Agnes and Kathy. I'm not laughing. I said I would like to have a meeting with you two Agnes, Kathy, me and someone else of higher authorities from the union. Please!, instead Agnes said no! more vitamins and I don't like the way you talked to Kathy. Kathy is the acting supervisor. Kathy didn't like that my personality had changed. I felt like my personality did not change. I would not have done anything like that. I don't think all that laughter was necessary.

Mr. De Aloes: What happened?

Marian: I waited and waited for several weeks No! The meeting date was assigned to take place. I went to talk to Agnes in her office. She gave me her rules and everything that she didn't want me to do anymore. She said that she was going to get at all the other people about some of the stuff that they had delivered there and she was putting a stop to all that.

Mr. De Aloes: Kathy told you that?

Marian: No! Agnes. Agnes did? I patiently waited for a meeting. Then she wrote me a counseling memo stating she wanted me to watch my behavior. So I went to talk to her in her office. I wasn't doing anything but coming to work and answering my console. I told Kathy I didn't want to work with all the TSR's anymore because of her behavior. She was the supervisor. Why all that laughing when I'm trying to talk to her seriously? So Agnes said she didn't like me saying what I had said to Kathy again. But I didn't spread rumors. I talked straight forward. I said I wanted a meeting, because I felt that Kathy was still making fun of me. That's the way I felt. I felt like Agnes took favors and favored Kathy by writing me up and not Kathy. So I went to the union to file a grievance. I feel like they all were playing favoritism in our office. But she liked the way I worked. I used to get 100 on my work performance evaluation every month. Now she said she didn't like my new conduct or behavior. I saw no! difference in my behavior.

Mr De Aloes: So you went to the union to file a grievance. When did you do that?

Marian: When I got the counseling memo on the eighteenth of March. A month later I went to the union. I don't remember the date, it was at the end of April. I met with the union representative named Brenda, in the cafeteria in the medical center. She told me that she was going to file my grievance, then she gave me a copy of the letter. She also said that she was going to call Agnes, to try to schedule a meeting between me, the union, Kathy and Agnes.

Mr. De Aloes: So what is the next thing that happened

Marian: Well! After we talked, I told her what I was going through in the office, as deep as the Agnes playing favorites and not scheduling a meeting, so we can come to an understanding. The union representative Brenda said to me Agnes didn't even call her. She also said when I'm not in my office, I'm working from home. Agnes didn't return my call. She does things like that. So I said, okay, but after several weeks I didn't hear from the union representative or my supervisor Agnes regarding anything. I called and left several messages. I wanted to know if I could see the grievance that was filed. I would like to know if I'm supposed to sign it, read it, get a copy or what

Mr. De Aloes: No! answer from Brenda?

Marian: I received no! answer, so I started putting in for other departments.

Mr. De Aloes: You mean, applying for other jobs? Transferring into another position.

Marian: Agnes posted the job postings when she felt like it. She is supposed to post them every Monday when they come out. Sometimes she didn't put them up at all. I would go into the office and I'd ask her for the job postings. I also complained to the personal representative Martha about how slow Agnes was about putting up the job postings. And Martha said Well, you can always come by my office Marian to pick up the latest job posting. Or you can walk over to the personnel office and read the postings okay! I believe she was playing favorites too. On April seventh I walked into the office, the chemical smell was all in the air. I said what's going on here? I'm getting sick. What is wrong? Linda said *(she's one of the older operators)*. Marian the carpets were cleaned and that's what you are smelling. The chemicals from the carpets. We cannot open our windows. I said. I can't work with this smell. I feel sick. We had caution signs all outside, because the building to the left of us was under new construction. It was being torn completely down. The men outside worked with masks on. The yellow tape is all around. I'm having an allergic reaction. I feel like I'm getting asthma too. Linda had the fan going, blowing all those chemicals in the air. I should have stayed home for two days.

Mr. De Aloes: Okay, this is just too much.

Marian: I couldn't stand it anymore. I asked Agnes when they were spraying the carpet for fleas, to call me so I can stay at home. I can't be around sprays and chemicals. They don't even spray my apartment, without letting me know. My apartment manager would tell you No! We don't spray because Marian suffers from allergies and asthma.

Mr. De Aloes: So! What was the upshot of what happened after the carpet got cleaned?

Marian: Agnes said they had the carpet cleaned, without warning anyone. So I left the office, that day I went and filed my first Workers Comp case. My head hurt so bad. I felt very stressed. I was asked at Stress Care, do you think you could go back to work? I said Please! Ma' am, please! I don't feel I can. She said well I'll help you. You will have to go without pay until Eden grants you disability. They have their own separate disability from state disability. So I filed medical leave without pay. I've been taking treatments ever since.

Mr. De Aloes: So what kind of problems did you start having as a result of this stress?

Marian: My head, throat, sinus pressure, neck, shoulders hurt, muscle spasms and irritable stomach nausea.

Mr. De Aloes: Any other symptoms? Let me change that question.

Marian: Well what do you mean?

Mr. De Aloes: Employment at Eden was different from any other employment that you may have ever experienced before?

Marian: Yes! They got on my nerves

Mr. De Aloes: The automobile accident back in 1973, did you ever have any problems with your neck?

Marian: No! Not after my physical therapy treatments. I didn't have any more problems with my neck.

Mr. De Aloes: So you didn't have anymore problems following that automobile accident of 1973?

Marian: No! No! No! I didn't have a back set, if that's what you're trying to say.

Mr. De Aloes: Are there any other complaints of conditions that you relate to your employment at Eden? Any other conditions to physical, mental symptoms?

Marian: They were totally disrespectful towards me, trying to make me feel I was no nobody. Playing on my self-esteem.

Mr. De Aloes: Did they succeed?

Marian: Yes! That's why I went to Stress Care. Mr. De Aloes Are you stereotyping me as a certain type of person? I wanted the same kind of respect that was being given to other employees.

Mr. De Aloes: No! I'm not stereotyping you. Do you think that you were mentally disabled as a result of the actions of Eden?

Marian: Yes! And I don't want to go back to that department at Eden. It made me so stressed, sir!

Mr. De Aloes: You're saying mentally and physically disabled. For how long? Do you have any problems with your mental functioning?

Marian: Let me make myself clear, in other words since I'm staying away from Eden, attending Stress Care I'm feeling better.

Mr. De Aloes: Will you please answer my questions?

Marian: Yes! I feel better. What do you mean? I don't know how long I'm going to take. Before I'm healed.

Mr. De Aloes: Would you be returning to work for Eden?

Marian: I would prefer another department, before I come back into that office. Something more peaceful.

Mr. De Aloes: How did you get referred to Stress Care?

Marian: I heard an announcement over the radio.

Mr. De Aloes: What radio station were you listening to when you heard the advertisement?

Marian: J. L. H. W. the announcer said, If you're feeling stressed, headache or you are having differences with your boss? stuff like that. Come see us and we'll take care of you. I said to myself, that's just what I'm going through.

Mr. De Aloes: Did you have a long wait before being seen?

Marian: No! I didn't have a long wait at all. At first I saw a gentleman named Victor. I don't know what his position was. Maybe he was the intake person. He asked me how I was feeling. Would I like to see a doctor? What symptoms was I having? And I told him. Then I saw a lady psychiatrist.

Mr. De Aloes: Did Victor take your history at all?

Marian: Yes! He did. He asked me, have I ever had a nervous breakdown or suffered from mental illness or been in an automobile accident before, or anything related to it. And I said yes! In 1975 and 1976 I was given forms and questionnaires. The first one was just two pages, but the second was a very long booklet.

Mr. De Aloes: Did Victor ask you questions about your personal and past history? in details

Marian: Yes! He wanted to know it all.

The doctor that you saw after Victor? What was her name? How much time did this doctor spend with you?

Marian: I don't remember her name. We probably talked for about thirty minutes. My feeling was at its worst. I needed help.

She asked me, could I go back to work while they contact Disability, because Eden is different, they don't go by state disability. I said please! I was not mentally or physically ready to go back into that office.

Mr. De Aloes: Did you see somebody else there?

Marian: No! Not that day. She filled out the papers and gave me copies to mail into the Eden Disability office by certified mail.

Mr. De Aloes: Did you respond to her spontaneously?

Marian: Yes! Just like I'm responding to you.

Mr. De Aloes: What's the next thing that happened?

Marian: She gave me an appointment to come back. And an appointment to go to their medical center Sheffield.

Mr. De Aloes: So you went straight to Sheffield from there?

Marian: Yes!

Mr De Aloes: Who was the person that you saw at Sheffield?

Marian: Dr. Stewart was the first doctor that I saw.

Mr. De Aloes: Where is Sheffield Medical located?

Marian: On the corner of Vermont and Province. I don't know their address. I forgot. I can look it up.

Mr. De Aloes: That's all right, they'll let us know. Were there many people waiting in the waiting room at Sheffield Medical?

Marian: Yes! But they took me in right away. I don't know! There were a lot of people there, but I told them, please! I can not sit down and wait. Nor can I fill out another form. They had someone else fill it out for me.

Mr. De Aloes: So that other person asked you questions and then filled out the form on your behalf?

Marian: Yes! They did and I signed it. I don't know who that person was.

Mr. De Aloes: How much time did they spend with you filling out that form?

Marian: I don't know! I don't know how much time. It must have been thirty minutes to an hour. I don't know! I doubt if it was an hour. Maybe thirty, forty minutes or less.

After that gentleman went over the form with you, you saw Dr. Stewart?

Marian: Yes! I saw Dr. Stewart and he started examining me and asking me my medical history.

Mr. De Aloes: How much time did Dr. Stewart spend with you?

Marian: Oh! let me guess. Maybe I stayed in there for an hour, because he gave me a physical. Examined my neck, my back, my ears, my nose, and my stomach. I don't know. I don't know for how long, or how many minutes.

Mr. De Aloes: Did he prescribe for you any medication that day?

Marian: He gave me something for my head.

Mr. De Aloes: Did he prescribe for you physical therapy?

Marian: Yes! My appointment for physical therapy was a week later. At Sheffield Medical clinic, prescribed twice a week.

Mr. De Aloes: What kind of therapy did you get?

Heat on my neck, back and shoulders, then my back was rubbed down with oil or some type of medication. Then the massaging machine was applied on my neck and my back. And medication was prescribed.

Mr. De Aloes: Do you know what kind of medication it was?

Marian: I've written it down on a piece of paper. Methocarbamol, M-e-t-h-o-c-a-r-b-a-m-o-l, Terfenadine, T -t-e-r-f-e-n-a-d-i-n-e.

Mr. De Aloes: So how long did each physical therapy session last?

Marian: About thirty minutes.

Are you still getting therapy?

Mr. De Aloes: Did the therapy help at all?

Marian: Yes! It eased a lot of tension.

Mr. De Aloes: Are you still seeing anybody at Stress Care?

Marian: No! Not at Stress Care. I finished the group therapy. They gave me some referrals, because the doctor still feels I should have some type of mental therapy counseling.

Mr. De Aloes: Did you have any individual therapy too?

Marian: Yes! Several times

Mr. De Aloes: How long did each individual session last?

Marian: About thirty to forty minutes, maybe an hour, where we just talked. Just me and the psychologist, nobody else was in there.

Mr. De Aloes: So let me backup because I'm a little confused. The actual sessions with the doctor herself lasted about thirty to forty minutes, maybe an hour, is that right?

Marian: Yes!

Mr. De Aloes: How many people participated in group therapy?

Marian: Maybe! Five or six. It was small.

Mr. De Aloes: Do you know who the person that ran the group sessions?

Marian: Joanna!

Mr. De Aloes: Do you know her last name?

Marian: No!

Mr. De Aloes: Do you know her credentials?

Marian: No! *Uh Uh hum*

Mr. De Aloes: Do you know if she was a psychologist or an MFCC?

Marian: She gave me a paper that she had written it on. I don't know her credentials, but she got some. And I don't know her last name.

Mr. De Aloes: Were all of the people in these group sessions worker's compensation claimants?

Marian: I believe so, yes!

Mr. De Aloes: And how many group sessions did you attend?

Marian: It's a total of ten group sessions. One was missed because of the riot. And one was missed because of my granddaughter's funeral. But I was at all the others. The day of the Los Angeles riot, the office was closed. It had a sign posted CLOSED. If I knew these questions were going to be asked, I would have brought more information than I did; but I didn't. I have never been to a thing like this before.

Mr. De Aloes: How did the sessions at Stress Care help you Marian?

Marian: Well! Joanna, she trained me to speak with compassion and respect for others. Think it over what you want to say. If I have to say something, Don't hold anything in. She said that would be a buildup, let it out. Speak your mind with compassion and respect for others. Don't sit there and work under high pressure and have all that in your head. You held too much, and you held it too long. I felt like she was telling me the truth.

Mr. De Aloes: You mentioned at the beginning of the deposition that your thoughts were on another court right now. What did you mean by that?

Marian: My granddaughter was killed on April twenty-second. My son's friend Ronald was hit by an automobile. He was holding her. He had just asked the baby's mother if he could see the baby. She was six months old. He was on the outside of the car. A car purposely swerved over and hit him, because he was wearing red tennis shoes.

Mr. De Aloes: Gang-type colors or something?

Marian: Yes! It was his red tennis shoes. Oh! He was not a boy. He was a man. The shoes ticked the young man in the blue off. He is having his court day today at 8:30 a.m. He purposely swerved his car and hit Ronald. Ronald goes up into the air with my granddaughter and she comes down on her head. They took her to Martin Luther King Hospital. She was classified as brain dead. The doctors said are you her grandmother as he approached me giving me her hair in a plastic bag, from her shaved head. They'd shave her hair trying to get her brain to respond. The doctor said that they would work with her for three days, to try to get her brain to function. After 3 days she was classified as brain dead. On the 4th day I went to the mortuary and quietly glued her hair back on and dressed her in clothes for her funeral. I had a hard time taking her foot out of my mouth, no more this little piggy went to the market. I was greeted by a UCLA Donor center representative who asked me, to help save other children's lives, by donating her internal organs. After carefully thinking I said yes! hoping to someday meet the children that have my granddaughter's internal organs inside.

Mr. De Aloes: I'm very sorry! Was she living at your house?

Marian: Yes! With her mother, her clothes are still there. But since this has happened, I've been grieving, I just wanted to sit. Sit at home and just go to treatment.

Mr. De Aloes: Who was Ronald, again?

Marian: Ronald is a friend of my son's. He was holding my granddaughter. He was holding my granddaughter in his arms at the time he was hit by a car.

Mr. De Aloes: Did Ronald sustain any injuries?

Marian: Yes! He was on crutches for a while. With 2 broken legs, chest and back injuries.

Mr. De Aloes: When did your granddaughter die?

Marian: She was classified dead April the twenty-fourth. We had her funeral on May 1st.

Mr. De Aloes: The person that hit Ronald and your granddaughter is on trial today in criminal court?

Marian: Yes! Downtown. They were supposed to have his arraignment this morning at 8:30 this morning in Division 45, at Criminal Court. At 500 Temple, or 250 Temple, 210 West Temple. I'm not sure of the address.

Mr. De Aloes: So this Deposition was obviously an upsetting experience.

Marian: Yes! It is. But I had already started my stress treatments before this happened. I thank God that I had the medicine that Dr. Stewart gave me, so I could go to sleep at night. I needed something to relax my nerves. Even when I got to Martin Luther King hospital they had to give me medication.

Mr. De Aloes: You got medication at Martin Luther King hospital while you were waiting for your granddaughter in critical care?

Marian: Yes! I needed something. When my son called me he was screaming hysterically, saying, Mama! Mama, come quick. The baby was hit by a car, they took her to Martin Luther King hospital. I didn't know what to think. This couldn't be his way of playing around for April Fool's. It was so painful I told him. Please! don't tell me anything like that. Then he said Mama please! come over here. I cannot explain the feeling that took over me as I drove my car, towards where my son and my granddaughter's mother were earlier that day. As I came near I saw a lot of police cars and a very large crowd of people. I saw he wasn't playing, that's when things just got worse. Everything thought in my head just got worse.

Mr. De Aloes: After you arrived on the scene, what happened?

Marian: I didn't want to talk to the police and stop them from their report. They were looking for answers just like me. I asked a boy who knew my son, he was on his bicycle. I said, hello! Do you know where my son is? And he said, He is walking around crying and screaming. He wouldn't let anybody touch him. Then I saw the police knocking at the doors, looking for witnesses. A Mexican guy was laying on the ground waiting for an ambulance, he was hit too. The car hit more than Ronald. It hit the Mexican guy too. Then I asked the garbage man who was a friend of my son, hello! What happened? The garbage man said, It was hit and run. The boy with a blue shirt drove his car into a few people, just to hit Ronald because he had on red tennis. It threw him up in the air, he was holding the baby, she went up, out from his arms and came down and hit her head on the ground. I lost my granddaughter. Sometimes she slept with me at night, I said. Do you know where my son is? I didn't know what to expect at this point. No! You have to look for him. He is probably around here somewhere. He didn't go to the hospital. He's crying, feeling really bad because he tried to catch the baby, but he missed catching the baby. He was on the other side of the car. And where is my granddaughter's mother? He said she rode with the ambulance to the hospital. I'd heard enough, so I drove on to Martin Luther King hospital. When I arrived I had to wait three hours before I could see her. I knew it was serious. Many of my family members had arrived too. The doctor told us to go sit in the chapel. And we all went to the chapel.

Mr. De Aloes: Which son was this?

Marian: Mr. De Aloes, I told you_ I only had one son. Nathaniel Junior, Just that one.

Mr. De Aloes: How old is he? He is nineteen.

Marian: My thoughts went hysterically crazy. I went back to the psychotherapist Joanna and I said do you think that somebody on my job had my granddaughter hit? Me, Agnes and Kathy weren't speaking friendly to each other. I remember Kathy's husband coming to our job one day about 5:20 p.m. wearing dark sunglasses, jeans and a t-shirt, with cut-off sleeves. I just felt like he was staring at me with dark sunglasses. I hate to think like this about a person, that intentions may be out to get me. I talked to Joanna about it and she said, No! He just probably came to pick her up from work. That's why I said I needed help with my thoughts. That's how weird I was thinking. She said No! Marian, don't go off with these thoughts. Stop! Stop! Why would they target your granddaughter? Why didn't they hit your son? Why didn't they come and hit you? *(I was thinking critically, hysterically, and bizarrely my head was totally wild.)* No! Marian, don't even think like that Joanna said. They wouldn't do anything like that.

Mr. De Aloes: Was Nathaniel a member of a gang?

Marian: Yes! But this wasn't a gang retaliation. He also knows a lot of gang members of different gangs that go to his school and that live in the neighborhood. He had also been a victim himself of a drive-by. And he has lost two of his cousins due to drive-bys. At their high school no one knows who did it nor did anyone want to talk about it. A car drove by and shot two teenagers standing at the hamburger stand. My son was shot in the leg. And they don't know who did it. South Central Los Angeles is known for drive bys, all types of gang fights, unexplainable killings and gang initiation killings.

Mr. De Aloes: When was your son shot?

Marian: Four years ago. I used to live in South Central, but I don't live in South Central anymore. My father was a victim. He used to work at USC Medical. His supervisor from USC Medical called my sister saying he hadn't called or reported to work for four days. He never did that before. His co-workers hadn't seen him since he got paid. We all knew he drank, but he still went to work. I remember my father calling me from a phone booth by his house, and told me, Marian I've been jumped, kicked in the stomach, and robbed by some boys, when I got off the bus. I asked are you ok? He said yes! I'm going home, going to have a drink, going to sleep, and going back to work in the morning. That was the last conversation I had with him. He never woke up. I thought that he went to work. Until I heard from my sister.

Mr. De Aloes: When was this?

Marian: This was in 1980, 1981

Mr. De Aloes: What was the cause of death?

Marian: The death certificate stated that he had internal bleeding and hardening of the liver and arteries. He told me that he had been jumped, robbed and kicked in the stomach.

Mr. De Aloes: So it sounds to me like he had a coronary following that?

Marian: Yes! They never knew, they never knew anything related to that accident either.

Mr. De Aloes: I'm sorry! They never followed or investigated anything when that happened.

Marian: No! with my granddaughter, the detective was going around doing an investigation. The funeral was covered by The Victims of Crime and donations from the public. I don't want them to tell me that they are going to let this young man go because nobody showed up. Because I had to come here today.

Mr. De Aloes: Is your mother still alive?

Marian: No! My mother died when I was 7.

Mr. De Aloes: Did your father ever remarry?

Marian: No! He never remarried. Deep down inside I was always afraid I missed my mother, so much during my childhood. I never trusted or wanted another mother. No! another woman could not take her place.

Mr. De Aloes: Do you have any brothers or sisters?

Marian: There's five children in my family. I have three sisters and one brother. I was always pranking and playing games with them.

Mr. De Aloes: Where are you along the chain of descent there?

Marian: I'm the second child.

Mr. De Aloes: Where did your siblings live?

Marian: Where? What? Siblings Live!

Mr. De Aloes: Your brothers and sisters? I mean, your sisters and brother.

Marian: Mr. De Aloes you're testing me. I've answered all your questions already. We move around ... My grandmother and my cousins got together and bought an apartment building in Brooklyn, New York. My youngest sister lives there. She has sickle cell, she loves to have fun and party. But we all move back and forth.

Mr. De Aloes: So your brother and sisters live in New York?

Marian: My brother lives in Los Angeles, county. He was angry with me for a long time, for popping boogers on his face, while eating oatmeal. When we were young. He said oatmeal looks like boogers in it and he didn't want to eat it. Marian, you are nasty. So he didn't visit me often.

Mr. De Aloes: You have children in New York too?

Marian: Yes! I told you my daughter Flawn'Telle lives in New York.

Mr. De Aloes: Do you have any other grandchildren?

Marian: Yes! How many? Flawn'Telle has three kids and Lishelle has two.

Mr. De Aloes: Have you ever seen any psychologist or psychiatrist in the past?

Marian: Yes! I did

Mr. De Aloes: When?

Marian: I had group therapy before in 1975, when I was pregnant with Mynisha. 1974 I had problems making a decision whether I wanted an abortion, and 1973 whether I wanted to marry David Burns or to deal with Jeff Lawrence, he did not want his twins I was carrying. And I was also sleeping with a married man I couldn't reveal. I went to group counseling regarding that. It was so much pain and a hurt feeling like being kicked and crushed. I went to a clinic in Oakland, CA

Mr. De Aloes: Do you recall the name of that clinic?

Marian: It was on East 14th, before Hegenberger Road. I don't know the name of it. I didn't file for job stress. I was working for the city of Oakland. It was at the courthouse and I was out on maternity leave. There wasn't any stress on my job. There were only three people in the office. The office wasn't stressful. It was just home stress.

Mr De Aloes: Is that the only time that you can remember getting any mental health treatment at all? Mental health treatment,

Marian: No! In 1974 and 1975 I heard voices, telling me I'm going to wash you and make you clean. I was washing myself 3 to 4 times a day. I was washing everything in my house and I was washing my children. I started reading bibles, pulling out bible pages and twisting bible pages, tying them in my Dread locked hair, stuffing them in my ears and I slept with my bibles in my bed. I didn't trust anyone. I remember cleaning and locking up my house I rented. Taking all my money out of the bank. Then me and my children caught a Greyhound bus to Los Angeles, CA. While riding on the bus, I heard more voices, telling me I was going to be killed. Get off Now! I was praying and chanting so loud the bus driver said I was very disturbing, maybe I needed to get off the bus and get some rest, so I did. I got off in Bakersfield, CA and rested. I didn't want anyone to know nor did I want to talk about that event in my life. My Aunt Coulda and 5 missionaries, my father and my cousin Gloria took me straight to Martin Luther Psychiatric hospital for evaluation. I was there overnight.

Mr. De Aloes: Were those the same feelings or events you were getting again uhumm.

Marian: No! That experience was different than I ever felt before. I've been waiting for my disability from Goldenseal, I was sitting home for two months without any kind of assistance or anything. I pawned all my jewelry, putting things in a pawn shop, because Goldenseal Insurance kept saying that the doctor's statements still needed questions answered. And he said that he answered them, and so no one could help me. So I went and applied for public assistance. I showed them all my paperwork and everything I had been through. Then I gave them copies of the medical records from Sheffield, Stress Care and my family death certificates. I talked to them and told them how stressful I was. Later I also called the deputy director's office and finally they helped me.

Mr. De Aloes: What are your monthly expenses?

Marian: My rent was $413 a month. I had an eviction at my door, but they didn't proceed with it.

Mr. De Aloes: Had what?

Marian: Before I called the deputy director's office I had an eviction notice. An eviction notice was posted? Yes! To move or pay my rent. I even called the Christian Conference. I talked to them and said Listen! I can't go back to work right now, I'm too stressed. And No! one is answering me with public assistance. I don't have any money. I've pawned everything for food.

Mr. De Aloes: Why did you call the Christian Conference?

Marian: I've been calling everybody. Churches, Travelers Aid Societies and every charity organization for help. That's how I found a little assistance, by calling the charity organizations. They were referring me from one to another. Due to the riot that was going on in Los Angeles. I told the receptionist please! Help! I'm not calling for rioter's assistance. I need help! My rent is due, my lights, my phone bill, I don't even have gas for my car. I feel mentally and physically unstable.

Mr. De Aloes: So when did the eviction notice get posted on your door?

Marian: Diane called me, she's the manager of the apartment building where I live. She said Marian, you are two months behind with your rent. We are going to have to give you an eviction notice unless you can come up with something to avoid it. I said let me call some of the charity organizations. They referred me to the Welfare Department Deputy Director office. After that they issued me an emergency check for my rent, so I wouldn't get evicted and they issued me some food stamps.

Mr. De Aloes: How much money did you get from that assistance? The first check was $499, the second $499, the third $535 and $138 in food stamps. It was for the whole time that I've been off work as of today's date.

Mr. De Aloes: So you got three rent checks?

Marian: No! Not all the same day, within that month, then $138 in food stamps?

Mr. De Aloes: What's the office that issued those checks?

Marian: AFDC St. Vernon office on Exposition Drive.

Mr. De Aloes: What governmental entity, or what governmental department is that?

Marian: County Welfare, the social worker also got the notice from Goldenseal Insurance. She said she would give Goldenseal a call.

Mr De Aloes: Do you have car payments?

Marian: No! I finished my car payments. I had no money for car insurance.

Mr. De Aloes: I'm sorry! You had no money for your car insurance. What happened?

Marian: *(I can't believe this attorney)* I had no money for my car insurance. I was four months behind. They didn't turn it off because I have a good payment record. I kept a good record with the phone company too. I always paid on time. I wrote to the supervisor and told them what had happened. I also sent in copies of the newspapers about my granddaughter death. Me and my son had made several calls to my daughter in New York and to my daughter in Delaware.

Mr. De Aloes: You were calling your daughters in New York and Delaware because of the death of your granddaughter?

Marian: Yes! We needed someone to talk to. About my job, my problems, everything that was going on. I never called so much before then. Talking about my job, how stressful it was at work, how at first it was so pleasant to work there and then it just turned into a nightmare. It seemed like everything that I liked to do the most, turned bitter. They knew I loved answering the TSR's and the console. But they would always call me off of it and say, do and do this and do that. Agnes, my Eden supervisor, assigned you to this today! I liked talking with the public. And every day she would call me off the console. I asked why don't you just let me sit here and do what I was hired to do. No! Marian, I want you to do this because you catch on faster than some of the other workers in the office. Other employees were asking me Marian, why are you working on special projects? I've been here longer than you and I don't do that. That's when I asked Agnes Why don't Linda do it?

Mr. De Aloes: Okay! Well what other expenses besides your phone bill, electricity, and car insurance and monthly rent do you have? How much do you spend a month on food?

Marian: My food bill is rather high. I spend about $300 to $400 on food, because I eat a lot of healthy foods; chicken, beef, turkey, fish, fruits, vegetables, along with supplements. like ginseng, bee pollen, Aloe Vera juice and gel, vitamin C crystals, calcium and wheat germs. All that stuff costs, so my food bill is high.

Mr. De Aloes: What other kinds of monthly expenses do you have besides your food bill?

Mr. Biloba: Counsel, can we go off the record for one second?

Counsel: Sure!

Mr. Biloba: I would like to take a five-minute break to call my office. And I needed a break. (*In 15 minutes we were back on the record.*)

Mr. De Aloes: What were you saying?

Marian: When they started helping me, with welfare my rent was reduced. My daughter worked ten hours a week, five hours at the hamburger stand on a Saturday and five hours on a Sunday at Walmart. Sometimes she works less. The highest of all of my expenses, food is the highest. Ummm Oh! the credit union. I borrowed $500. from the credit union. I owed my operation. Then my son went through food poisoning. I owe the medical center a co-pay of $230., because he was hospitalized for twenty-four hours.

Mr. De Aloes: What was the food poisoning deal all about?

Marian: He last ate at the hamburger stand then he came home and fell on my bed and said, Mama, take me to the hospital. I said, What's wrong? he said, I don't know. Take me to the hospital. I feel sick. The doctors gave him a blood and urine test, pumped his stomach and monitored him all night. I had Health Net medical insurance. So they charged Health Net $2,000.00 and $230. copay to me. Plus I have dental expenses copay for my daughter. I owe the anesthesiology department for my operation. I paid the whole bill for my operation. But the medical center finance department made a mistake and sent me part of the money back. They thought I had paid too much. They sent me a check for six hundred dollars. Then they wrote me back a letter and said I owe the anesthesiology department $600 plus dollars. Well! I said, Why? I paid everybody. I paid the whole medical center bill before the operation. But the medical center finance department said that they had reimbursed me when they should have sent it to the Anesthesiology Department. This was in regards to my breast implants.

Mr. De Aloes: How much do you owe at the credit union?

Marian: $500.

Mr. De Aloes: What credit union is that?

Marian: Eden Telecommunications.

Mr. De Aloes: What are your current symptoms right now?

Marian: Well! Right now I feel relaxed and tired of so many questions. That's why I was saying I want to go back to another department part time or on call. So I don't have any more relapses. I talked to the landlord where I live and she said that they will always adjust my rent to my income, because she knows what I went through. She was there to see this. When I filed for job stress I had to go talk to her. I said Please! I know my rent is coming up, but something is going on. I don't know what's going on. I don't even understand myself.

Mr. De Aloes: So you're ready to go back to work?

Marian: The doctor and all my therapists said after the nineteenth. Mr. Biloba told me that he is sending a letter to Goldenseal on the nineteenth. That would be the last day for his services. I feel a lot of the tension has gone that was work-related.

Mr. De Aloes: Do you think you still have some residual stress because of the death of your granddaughter and all of the stuff that was going on?

Marian: Yes! Yes! I do. I'm not going to lie to you, I do. That was a great loss to me and a great amount of stress that I went through.

Mr. De Aloes: Do you think that would prevent you from going back to work?

Marian: No! No! That wouldn't prevent me from going back to work.

Mr. De Aloes: You think work might actually help you get over that a little bit?

Marian: I don't think work will help me get over that, but I think in time I will get over it. I still feel stressful when it comes down to the event of her loss, and I feel worse when I think about it all over again.

Mr. De Aloes: I'm not following?

Marian: At my job we had special things we did, if something happens to anyone or their family member. The supervisor will get a card and she passes it around so everyone could sign it, if it's a congratulation or a death.

Mr. De Aloes: Marian what would you do if they passed around a card? Would you sign it?

Marian: I don't think so. I wouldn't participate in it. I wouldn't participate with the parties either. And as far as anything coming into that office, I told Agnes I wouldn't order a hot dog to be delivered there. Debbie and my other co-workers sent me a sympathy card though.

Mr. De Aloes: Getting back to the symptoms: do you have any symptoms now that you attribute to your job stress?

Marian: No! because I haven't had anybody bothering me. A letter came from Martha, our personal supervisor, stating that my grievance was denied. I took the letter and I folded it up, put it in my purse. One week passed, and then she called me. She said Marian, why didn't you call me and appeal it? I said why did you want me to call and appeal it? She said I didn't have all the facts. I figured she was waiting for me to call to see what my reaction was going to be after the denial, I didn't react. I said Martha, at a time like this in my life, I don't want to think about Eden. She said are going to appeal it? You have time to appeal, you know. I said No! I'm not. I'm grieving. I don't want to appeal it.

Mr. De Aloes: Martha is the union rep. Right?

Marian: No! She is not. Martha is the personnel supervisor. I felt like Marian, if you file an appeal, you're not going to do anything but lose. Because they are playing with me again. I have the denial letter right here. They were playing with me and I was grieving. I'm not going to play the game with them again. They didn't even return my call to Mr. De Aloes. I called Martha several times before and said, will you please! send my benefit documents to the doctor office so that they can send it to Goldenseal insurance company. That's the only thing that I had to say to her. They didn't think I was serious.

Mr. De Aloes: So what do you want out of this worker's compensation case?

Marian: Well

Mr. De Aloes: What are you expecting to accomplish by this worker's compensation case?

Marian: First of all, I would like to be transferred to another department. Where the people are more serious minded. I would like my workers compensation claim settlement to pay for my days I was not working receiving treatments for pain and suffering. And I would like for Goldenseal to stop playing, because the doctor has answered them.

Mr. De Aloes: Is there anything that you used to be able to do that you can't do now as a result of the problems that you've experienced at Eden?

Marian: You know what, to tell you the truth, mentally I feel that I've gotten stronger, because I will be able to speak out more faster. As far as the problems with them. I have not really gotten them solved. I would say no! I can do everything.

Mr. De Aloes: I don't have any other questions.

Marian: (*Softly in my inner voice I don't believe it, Mr. De Aloes has no more questions for me. Oh! And it's finally Mr. Biloba turn uh hmm, this is almost over.*)

Mr. Biloba: Counsel! I just have a few short questions for Ms. Dorsey Marian! We have reviewed some forms at my office in preparation for today's deposition. Do you recall that? Yes! Let me show you this first form which is called Employee's Claim for Worker's Compensation Benefits. Online seven it says, Signature of employee. Is that in fact your signature Marian?

Marian: Yes!

Mr. Biloba: And you signed this yourself. Is that correct?

Marian: Yes!

Mr. Biloba: I would like to ask that this be entered as applicant's exhibit number one, a copy of which you should have. Secondly is a form which is called a Disclosure Statement. Do you recognize this form?

Marian: Yes! I even remember that conversation.

Mr. Biloba: And on the form it has a place for employee signature. Is that in fact your signature?

Marian: Yes! It is.

Mr. Biloba: And I see a date of July 7, 1992. Is that your date?

Marian: Yes!

Mr. Biloba: I would like to ask that this be entered as applicant's exhibit number two, the disclosure statement. Additionally, we have two forms that we use in my law office. On this first form, we have filled in the complaints or symptoms in regards to your worker's compensation claim. Do you recognize the form?

Marian: Yes!

Mr. Biloba: And here we can see the applicant's signature. Is that in fact your signature?

Marian: Yes!

Mr. Biloba: And we can see a date of seven hyphen seven hyphen ninety-two. Did you date this, Marian?

Marian: Yes!

Mr. Biloba: And one of my staff, Joe Donald, assisted you in completing this form. Is that correct?

Marian: Yes!

Mr. Biloba: Where we see up here lines one through eleven is that in fact, your handwriting?

Marian: Yes!

Mr. Biloba: And the subsequent lines, one through four is that additionally your handwriting?

Marian: Yes!

Mr. Biloba: Thank you! I would like to ask that this be entered as applicant's exhibit number three, and last we have a form that we use in the office which is a picture of a human anatomy. Do you recognize the form, Marian?

Marian: Yes!

Mr. Biloba: And where it says, signature is that, in fact, your signature?

Marian: Yes! That's my signature.

Mr. Biloba: And we see a date of seven hyphen seven hyphen ninety-two. Is that your handwriting?

Marian: Yes!

Mr. Biloba: And I can see that there are various parts of the diagram that have been marked off, circled or marked with an "X." Did you, in fact, personally make those marks?

Marian: Yes! I did.

Mr. Biloba: Thank you! I would like to ask that this be entered as applicant's exhibit number four. I wouldn't have any further questions.

Counsel: Would you like to redirect in reference?

Mr. Biloba: I have no further questions.

Marian: I sat quietly as the Counsel proposed to relieve the court reporter of her duties. Listening as he stated the original transcript booklet, can be directed to Mr. Biloba office. Well Mr. De Aloes took me through several painful hours of questions, pulling at my haunted past, trying to confuse my thoughts, twisting and tangling my words. A wake up call, my deposition, of an awakening experience.

Finally on October 8, 1992 Goldenseal Insurance mailed a check to Mr. Biloba for; Stress Care, Sheffield Medical Center and me. I received $2,045.88 for twelve weeks of disability. After recovering from some of my emotional stress, I tried to return back to work. But I was told by Eden's insurance company that all the doctors' paperwork for my clearance to return to work, still wasn't in yet. So I was left without a job. I was forced to file for my unemployment benefits. Before the final court date Mr. Biloba called me saying he was suspended from the state bar, Sheffield Medical Center was closed down. Could I come in and pick up my deposition transcript? Yes I said, I may want to add it to my book that I'm writing.

January 17, 1994 Claude Hudson Clinic discovered a mass in my breast, during my yearly mammogram, they referred me to USC Medical Center Cancer Clinic. Several x-rays were given to me. I had to undress down to my waist and stand up right against the x-ray machine. While the radiology technologist took one of my breasts at a time. She carefully separated the breast pulling it in front of the implant and positioned my breast pressing it with her hands against the x-ray machine. Swiftly moving her hands as the x-ray machine moved a plate to take the place of her hands. The plate continued pressing my breast firmly against the x-ray machine for a few seconds. Boy! did that hurt... Then the radiology technologist went into a booth in the same room to shield herself from the radiation. She told me to hold my breath as she took the pictures of the x-rays of my breast.

The x-ray images created pictures of the inside of my breast, so the doctors could see lumps inside. The results of my x-rays showed, I'd developed lumps in my upper right breast. Then I was scheduled for a needle directed breast biopsy. Where I laid on an operating table. The technologist used my x-ray images to pinpoint where the lumps were with needles. I was put to sleep by an anesthesiologist. When I woke up I saw the doctor had made an inch and a half cut on my right breast to perform my biopsy operation, to remove the lump. And tissue samples were taken out of my breast and sent to the lab, which revealed a benign diagnosis. My results were not cancer.

After the biopsy, the right one appeared smaller. I felt like the right breast implant was leaking saline. Within the next few days the right breast implant was totally deflated. The doctor ruptured the right implant during the biopsy operation. So I had to get on the waiting list at Harbor UCLA Plastics Department on the ATP program based on patient ability to pay for the implants to be removed. Because the USC Medical Plastics department didn't want to get involved with the litigation. And I could no longer afford to go to the Medical Center, where I got them put in.

Finally July 5, 1995 the implants were removed. My breasts were cut open from the chest to the nipple to take out the implants. My scars were very bad. And my breast totally deformed. My right nipple was totally inverted, both breasts had dimples, the scars on both breasts were terrible. I suffered from muscle spasms. And I fell into a deep depression. I'd been writing to McGhee Medical Corporation, keeping them informed.

On July 18, 1995, two weeks after my surgery, Harbor UCLA Pathology Department called me to pick up the implants. I did just that. Then I called McGhee Corporation which immediately sent Federal Express over to my apartment to pick them up. I wanted a refund. September 6, 1995 McGhee Corporation called me to pick up the package. My implants which they cleaned, wrapped in a paper towel, placed in individual baggies and a letter of denial for a refund or any financial assistance.

Once again I had to start therapy for depression at Harbor Clinic. A few months later a Harbor Clinic doctor, who was an intern in plastics, heard about me. He called to offer me a breast reconstruction operation free to take place on December 20, 1995, for his class final. I had to sign an agreement which stated that if my nipples were lost during surgery, I would be substituted with tattooed ones. Wow! I was grateful nothing was lost! He even wanted to put in new implants, so they could appear identical again. But I said No! Because they looked much better, then they were. With a minimal amount of scares.

Throughout all of this I continued going to group therapy and one on one psychological therapy sessions. Until I recovered from depression. Then I tried appealing to get my job back, appearing in court several times without a lawyer, because no lawyer wanted to handle my case, figuring it wouldn't be enough money to compensate. I finally stopped my lawsuit against Eden and left with all my case papers in my hands.

Starting From the Ghetto

I'm starting from the ghetto, trying to reach the top. Climbing isn't very easy. I suffered from a drop. My mother died and her soul went to heaven when I was seven and my father died in nineteen eighty.

My loves weren't all laughter, being barefoot with four kids from the guys who stopped for a hop I walked over to my mirror, took a good look at my naked body, I knew it was time to stop. My soul was crying and my flesh was not satisfied with what my eyes had seen. At twenty-four my youthful breasts had fallen and my stomach was full of stretch marks. Memories in my mind of Grandmama, constantly reminding me "If a man can get the milk free why would he buy the cow?" In the ghetto where everyone plays a game I didn't want to be a street lady at night. Being successful, married with children was my aim to claim. Writing and music was my relief from pain. There's no room in the ghetto for me. I'm trying to reach the top.

Awakening Experience

I still heard voices inside my head which led me venturing into Open Mic's night at clubs and special events. I met a music producer, he offered me the opportunity to go into his recording studio for 3 days, 3 hours each day. When I arrived I took my wig and shoes off and we enjoyed ourselves. I was able to really let go and release all my inner voices. This was the beginning of my album Awakening Experience.

GOD'S POWER

I am Spirit inside my cell One so beautiful so rare Feel touch and share Life into power Listen to the birds singing Looking up at the sky Midnight blue mixed with gray Spirit of power God's power Feel touch and share Life into power God's power has fire God's power has fire Feel touch and share One so beautiful so rare Feel touch and share Life into power, God's power God's power, God's power

GOD'S POWER 3000

Ahm, ahm, deeper than my ears could hear Deeper than my eyes could see Deeper than my heart could feel Ahm, life reach out and feel Deeper than my eyes could see Deeper than my ears could hear Deeper than my heart could feel Reach out and feel Life into power, reach out and feel Feel touch and share Feel touch and share Feel touch and share

Feel touch and share Feel touch and share Life into power You got to reach out and feel You got to reach out and feel Life into power Feel touch and share Feel touch and share Life into power real power

I'VE GOT A LOT TO SAY

The suspense is killing me I'm worried I've meditated my thoughts until I've forgotten or I just can't think As I let the spirit flow I feel in my heart he wants to see me Thinking positive of our last conversation Well it's Tuesday I miss him in such a sweet way Trying to communicate through the third world sixth sense I can't stand no more no more suspense It's free to call God he's always there With someone or two on the line I'm on my way, *I feel I've got a lot to say* Well God, I'm on my way *I feel I've got a lot to say I'm on my way I feel I've got a lot to say* I'm on my way *I feel I've got a lot to say* Well God *I'm on my way I feel I've got a lot to say Hello God I'm calling You* Repeat 8 more times

INNER FEELINGS

Inner feelings deep within Are natural feelings that haven't just begin Inner feelings deep within Are natural feelings that haven't just begin I'm expressing them the best way I can Inner feelings I let my thoughts flow If I don't, I will be playing a game A game of being uncertain about the real me Inner feelings deep within Are natural feelings, that haven't just begin Inner feelings deep within Are natural feelings, that haven't just begin Inner feelings deep within Are natural feelings, that haven't just begin Inner feelings deep within Are natural feelings, that haven't just begin
Should I be playing about the real me
I should not be playing about the feelings I have inside of me Inner feelings deep within, inner feelings deep within Are natural feelings that haven't just begin Stop playing with these feelings inside I can't hide, should I play these feelings inside Should not, should not, should not, should not hide my feelings inside Inner feelings tell me deep within are natural feelings I just

begin, inner feelings deep within Tell me what to do with these feelings Tell me what to do with these feelings inside Thank God, I can't hide, show me, show me what to do I don't know what to do unless you show me what to do I don't, I don't know where to hide, I don't know what to do, do, Lord Should I, should I, what Lord, show me Lord, I can't hide

JUNE GONE GANGSTER

Mothers, fathers beware of what you use Because your sons and daughters will some day pay the dues Both gone wrong, tried to make a change, but no gain, no gain Trapped in this world of drugs, sex and pain Mothers, fathers, beware of what you use Because your sons and daughters will some day pay the dues Should have cared, more about my baby within Took it serious when, the doctor slapped him on his behind June gone gangster His opened eyes made his face shine June gone gangster Before his very first cry, he tried to hit him in the eye June gone gangster June gone gangster Squeezed the nurse that announced his birth June gone gangster He wasn't born ready to conquer the earth June gone gangster June gone gangster June gone gangster So mothers and fathers, beware of what you use Because your sons and daughters will some day pay the dues June gone gangster, June gone gangster Both gone wrong, tried to make a change, but no gain, no gain June gone gangster Trapped in the world of drugs, sex and pain June gone gangster June gone gangster So Mothers, fathers, beware of what you use Because your sons and daughters will some day pay the dues June gone gangster June gone gangster I Love ya, owe ya too, June, so sorry you had to pay the dues June gone gangster June gone gangster I Love ya, owe ya too, June gone gangster June so sorry you had to pay the dues June gone gangster June gone gangster I love ya, owe you too June gone gangster I love ya, owe you too Love ya

LET THERE BE LIGHT

This is the day the Lord has made We'll be glad and rejoice in it I don't believe in black magic I don't believe in astrologies Or the things this world has to offer I believe in God in me Let there be light Let there be light God saw it was good God saw it was good

La la la la la la la la la la la la la

Repeat 5 more times

God saw it was good God saw it was good This is the day the Lord has made We'll be glad and rejoice in it I don't believe in black magic I don't believe in astrologies Or the things this world has to offer I believe in God in me Let there be light Let there be light God saw it was good God saw it was good

La la la la la la la la la la la la la Repeat 13 more times

LETS PRAY TODAY

Background Vocals: *Do it, do it, do it, do it, do it, do it, do it, do it, do it, do it, do it Let's pray today, Let's pray today, Let's pray today Do it, do it, do it Let's pray today, Do it do it do it, Lets pray today, Do it, do it, do it Let's*

pray today, Do it, do it, do it, yeah, Lets pray today, Do it, do it
Our Father in Heaven,
Let's pray today, Do it, Do it, Let's pray today
Hallowed be your name, *Do it, Do it*
Your kingdom come, *Do it, Do it*
Your will be done
Do it, Do it, Let's pray today, Let's pray today
On Earth as it is in Heaven
Do it, do it, do it
Give us today our daily bread *Do it, do it, do it*
Forgive us our debts, *Let's pray today*
As we have forgiven our debtors
Do it, Do it, Do it, Do it
And lead us not into temptation *Lets pray today*
But deliver us from the evil one
Do it, Do it, Do it, Do it Let's pray today, let's pray today
Do it, do it, do it, yeah Lets pray today Let's pray today
Let's pray today Do it, do it Do it, Do it Let's pray today
Lets pray today Let's pray today

Our Father in Heaven Hallowed *Let's pray today*
Be your name Your kingdom come Your will be done On
Earth as it is in Heaven
Do it, do it, do it Let's pray today
Give us today *Let's pray today*
Our daily bread *Do it, do it, do it*
Forgive us our debts as we have also
Let's pray today
Forgiven our debtors And lead us not into temptation
Let's pray today
But deliver us from the evil one
Let's pray today, Let's pray today, Let's pray today Do it, do it, do it, Let's pray today, Do it, do it, do it Let's pray today, Do it, do it, do it, Lets pray today, Do it, do it, do it Let's pray today, Do it, do it, do it, yeah, Let's pray today, Do it, do it

SECRET LOVE

Concealed from my soul, the way my blood flows,

Mind and heart I hide inside the love I had for you from the start
Your present ignites my sight, smell, taste and touch
Yet it still grows like a forbidden fruit of a multitude of blessings I learn my life's lessons
Through grace that matures without a question of doubt
Making me want more of your love
I have to let my love for you out
Making me want more of your love
Not wanting to pretend you're just my friend
Making me want more of your love
Rehabilitating my thoughts of no regrets
I was confused about the pain I felt
Making me want Making me want more of your love
When your helping hand was revealed
More of your love
From my soul, the way my blood flows
Making me want more of your love
Mind and heart
More of your love

We took that start
Making me want more of your love
To express something that's so rare That we share
When no one's there Continuing to conceal an
understanding so real
God said come unto me
We were joined together unrehearsed
Give me your mind and heart
I took a bite out of my life's curse I isolated my soul
Give me your mind and heart Marian
The way my blood flows
Come unto me Mind and heart, *Come unto me*
And let mother nature's performance, her perfect works
of art
Destined the power of fate our karma will achieve
What people choose not to believe
Everyday satanic spirits play They try to mess up my
whole day
Making me want more of your love
God they're *Making me want more your love,*

God they're *Making me want more Making me want more Making me making me want more your love, love, everyday*
I'll seek your face, I'll seek your face, I'll seek your face

Savage Instincts

I want to be in love, I want to be loved
Secretly wondering and waiting to feel love
Desperately starving to be in love
Savage instincts tried to easily persuade me
Think wisely before you let go
Bad decisions, memories hurt over love
Fussing and fighting bit cha hate bite cha
And shame lick ya over love
I want to be in love, I want to be loved
Just to taste milk n honey love
Secretly wondering and waiting to feel love
Desperately starving to be in love
Savage instincts tried to easily persuade me
Think wisely before you let go

Candles incense fill the room
Music softly playing so gently
Feeling your wild savage beast next to mine
Just to taste milk and honey love
Secretly wondering and waiting to feel love
Desperately starving to be in love
Savage instincts tried to easily persuade me
Think wisely before you let go
Bad decisions, memories that hurt
Fussing, Fighting, Just to taste
We're all born with savage instincts
Hiding so deeply
Just to taste milk and honey love

My Conclusion Defining Myself

Sometimes we don't know why we do the things we do. Like our habits, we pick up or Genealogy we learn about. Or the words we select to use. How we use the cross, a rabbit foot, good luck charms or a worry stone, alcohol or drugs. We may have seen our parents, grandparents, aunts, uncles, cousins, friends or strangers, do something unusual to get them through a tough yet difficult time. Before I drive or participate in any activities. I pray, then I like to rub my cross and keep a prayer cloth on me.

I once asked my grandmother why she flushed our hair left in the comb and brush in the toilet and she said "So the birds won't pick it out of the trash and use your hair in her nest." I laughed without giving it a second thought. Now I flush the old hair from my comb and brush in the toilet. A habit I picked up from my grandmother I still do today.

I do not believe in witchcraft voodoo. Because if you believe it exists then it can happen to you. I believe in God. And I like to accept each person individually. No! two fingerprints are the same and no two individuals are the same. Everyone you meet has a different personality. But similarities may resemble, for those who believe in zodiac signs.

I had to feel my way through a lot of people in my life. I've been searching for true love and a mutual understanding. Often I choose the wrong lovers in my life. I found myself being too submissive, because I didn't like to be lonely. I Just want to have some fun and live a Holistic life. Well! About now you may think I'm still mentally unbalanced but I'm not. I'm an Artist and a Storyteller. I designed my arts, stories, poems, and songs to educate and entertain you.

Made in the USA
Columbia, SC
19 April 2023

12f71b8a-9dbd-48b6-8187-1ab00be577efR01